ICELANDIC MAGIC

Icelandic Magic

Icelandic Magic

Aims, tools and techniques of the Icelandic sorcerers

Christopher Alan Smith

PUBLISHED BY AVALONIA

www.avaloniabooks.co.uk

Published by Avalonia

BM Avalonia
London
WC1N 3XX
England, UK
www.avaloniabooks.co.uk

ICELANDIC MAGIC
Copyright © 2015 Christopher Alan Smith

First Edition, September 2015
(Paperback)

ISBN 978-1-905297-93-1

Cover image: Luck Knot from Lbs 2413 8vo. Reproduced with kind permission from the National and University Library of Iceland. Interior illustrations and images as credited.

Design by Satori, for Avalonia.

British Library Cataloguing in Publication Data. A catalogue record for this book is available from the British Library.

ABOUT THE AUTHOR

Christopher Alan Smith was born in Nottingham in 1954. He has travelled widely and lived in the Netherlands for five years, where his innate talent for languages enabled him to speak fluent Dutch within a few months and work as a logistics coordinator for a major transport company. His travels also include three visits to Iceland; on the second visit, he stayed in the country for 8 months and worked as a volunteer at the Museum of Icelandic Sorcery and Witchcraft in Hólmavík.

Christopher's interest in magic began when he was a student at the University of Sheffield, at which time the main emphasis in the available literature was on the Western Tradition of Kabbalistic magic. However, his taste for travel, languages and a restless search for knowledge clearly indicated Woden as his example, leading him within a few years towards Rune Magic and ultimately to membership of the Rune Gild. His Fellowship Work for the Gild, "The Icelandic Tradition of Magic" was published in 2012 as part of the collection "Occult Traditions" (Numen Books). In 2014 he was awarded the title of Master in the Rune Gild for his Master-work "Icelandic Magic in the Early Modern Period", which forms the basis of this book.

As he wryly comments in the introduction, "As my sixtieth birthday was approaching, I realised that I should perhaps have started on this project about forty years ago, beginning by studying Icelandic and folklore at university instead of politics… but one has to start somewhere."

Today he lives in North Yorkshire and, when not practising and researching Icelandic magic, works as a freelance translator.

ACKNOWLEDGEMENTS

Thanks are due to many people for their help in the completion of this book. Firstly, I thank my parents, who gave me a taste of knowledge and the best education that I was capable of absorbing. I also thank my friends and colleagues in the Rune Gild (especially my former Master and mentor, Dave Lee) for their interest and encouragement, and for providing many helpful references. In particular, I would like to thank the following individuals, some of whom are Gild members and others not:

Steve Wehmeyer, Michael Moynihan, Michael Putman, Kees Huyser and Mark Patton, for pointing me to many useful resources; my fellow researcher Justin Foster, who has shared much of his own material with me; Sverrir Guðmundsson, Ingibjörg Benediktdóttir, Benedikt (Bjössi) Petursson and Signý Olafsdóttir for helping with the translation of the Huld Manuscript; Alaric Hall for his advice and for obtaining photographic copies of two manuscripts; Sigurður Atlason, curator of the Museum of Icelandic Sorcery and Witchcraft, for his help and kindness when I worked as a volunteer at the museum; Magnús Rafnsson for patiently answering many questions with regard to his book 'Tvær Galdraskræður'; Terry Gunnell for his advice on aspects of Icelandic folklore; Matthew Driscoll of the

Arnamagnaean Institute for promptly providing me with digital copies of AM 434 12mo; my friend Damon Lycourinos for his encouragement and unwavering faith in my abilities as a researcher; and, last but not least, my partner Laurie for prodding me to stick to the task and for ensuring that I had the time to devote to the project.

Acknowledgements with regard to the illustrations:

All images derived from the manuscripts Lbs 143 8vo, Lbs 2413 8vo, Lbs 764 8vo and ÍB 383 4to (the 'Huld MS') are reproduced with kind permission of the National & University Library of Iceland. All images from AM 434 12mo 'Lækningakver' are reproduced with kind permission from the Arnamagnæan Institute in Copenhagen and its photographer Suzanne Reitz. The images from ATA, Ämbetsarkiv 2, F16:26 'Isländska Svartkonstboken' (Photographer: Bengt A. Lundberg), generally referred to in the text of this book as 'the Stockholm MS', are reproduced with kind permission from the Swedish National Heritage Board.

Icelandic Magic

TABLE OF CONTENTS

Icelandic Magic

INTRODUCTION

More than any other country, perhaps, Iceland has an iconic status for students of ancient Germanic lore and culture. The reasons for this are not hard to seek. The environment itself is dramatic, the perfect setting for tales of heroism and magic. A sub-Arctic island, oft-times battered by the cold waves of the North Atlantic Ocean and storms from the polar region, it is a land of glaciers and volcanoes where the primal forces of fire and ice compete to increase the hardship of the small population. Summers are brief and winters long, while spring and autumn struggle to find any place at all among the seasons. Arable land is hard to find, and even good grazing is at a premium. The earth itself shakes and rumbles from time to time. It is a land of liminality, where the world of men is squeezed and constricted between vast and hostile forces.

Remarkably, however, Iceland is less famous for its geography than for the vast outpouring of literature that its people have produced, especially in the Middle Ages. The very word 'saga', meaning 'story', has passed into English to denote a tale that is epic and heroic. From the earliest settlement at the end of the ninth century, Icelanders developed, passed on, and eventually recorded the tales of their lives, first by oral tradition and eventually through the establishment of a strong tradition of vernacular literacy. The written word was highly prized, and even today Iceland has the highest percentage of published authors per head of population in the world. It is mainly thanks to this vast output of literature, much of it written about two centuries after the country accepted Christianity, that we can form an idea about the pre-Christian beliefs, social customs and religious practices of our Germanic ancestors.

Another factor is that the people of Iceland jealously guard and preserve their culture. Though predominantly Lutheran by religion these days, they are as familiar with the mythic tales of Thor and Odin as they are with tales from the Bible. Even young children are taught at school to recite "Þat mælti mín móðir", the first poem of the famous Viking, poet and sorcerer Egill Skallagrímson. The Icelandic language has changed little over the past thousand years, certainly in comparison to its linguistic relatives in Scandinavia, the European mainland and the English-speaking world, and the country's educational establishment does its best to prevent the adoption of foreign words. Furthermore, belief in the old Germanic pantheon is making a modest comeback and, although the ratio is still small, Ásatrú – belief in the Æsir – is an officially recognised religion with a growing number of adherents. One can therefore certainly speak of a 'living tradition' that is more than of merely antiquarian interest.

From the elaborate sagas of the Middle Ages to the folk tales and legends collected and recorded by Jón Árnason in the nineteenth century, the stories of Iceland are shot through with magic and dealings with supernatural beings such as elves, land-wights, ghosts and trolls. Even today, many Icelanders attach credence to the continued presence of the 'hidden folk'; even if they do not absolutely believe in elves, they would not go so far as to categorically deny their existence. It has even been known for a major road to be diverted so as to avoid disturbing a place where the hidden folk are reputed to have their home. Of particular interest, in terms of magical practice, is the Strandir district of the Westfjords Region. Although this formerly remote and inaccessible area does not feature greatly in the sagas, its inhabitants came to acquire a reputation for prowess in the magical arts by the seventeenth century, and in 1930 a variant of the magic sign 'Ægishjálmur' (Helm of Awe, or Helm of Aegir) was adopted as the official emblem of Strandir. To capitalize on this aspect of local history and boost tourism, the Museum of Icelandic Sorcery and Witchcraft (Galdrasýning á Ströndum) was founded in 2000 at Hólmavík, the district's main population centre. The museum focuses on the 17th Century, when the European fashion for persecuting witches and sorcerers found its way to Iceland, with the result that a number of individuals were tried, convicted and punished with various degrees of severity. The museum houses an eclectic and fascinating collection of exhibits illustrating magical practices at that time: the 'Tilberi', a kind of vampiric worm; the 'sea mouse' (captured in order to gain money); a fish's head raised on a pole in order to control the winds; and, of course, the world-famous *Nábrók* or 'necropants'. It also has a display of reproductions of the grimoires that have survived the age of persecution and are now preserved in the National Library and the Arni Magnusson Institute in Reykjavik.

These grimoires (*galdrabækur*, or 'books of magic') in the Icelandic National Library and the Arni Magnusson Institute, together with other old manuscripts relating to runes and magic, are, or certainly should be, of great interest to anyone with a serious interest in the authentic practicalities of Germanic magic. They are certainly not hidden from view, as many of them have been catalogued on the website www.handrit.is together with others in the Arnamagnaean Institute in Copenhagen, and even made available as digitized copies, which one can download. So far, I have been able to identify 21 such manuscripts, and there are almost certainly more of them waiting to be listed. The earliest, AM 434 a 12mo 'Lækningakver' dates from between 1475 and 1525; the most recent, 'Rún', dates from 1928. In addition, there is the intriguing publication 'Galdraskræða' from 1940, in which Jochum Eggertsson, writing under the pen-name 'Skuggi', collated and presented the material contained in some of the manuscripts. This has recently been republished in hardback and in a somewhat different format.

Given the availability of this material, it comes as something of a surprise that nobody has yet attempted a comprehensive survey of Icelandic magic in the early modern period. Much has been written about magic and witchcraft in the Middle Ages, but most of these works tend to focus on the anthropological, ethnographic or sociological perspectives without much consideration for the practicalities, the 'nuts and bolts' if you like, of magic in northern Europe. François-Xavier Dillmann, in his monumental work "Les Magiciens dans l'Islande Ancienne" (2006), has made an extensive study of Icelandic magicians based on the saga literature, but he devotes only one chapter to how they actually proceeded in their work. Dr Stephen E. Flowers has translated and published one Icelandic grimoire contained in the Swedish national archives, together with commentary and some appendices based on an earlier, secondary work, under the title "The Galdrabók" (1989). Matthías Sæmundsson (1954-2004) published two books, "Galdrar á Íslandi. Islensk galdrabók" (1992) and "Galdur á brennuöld" (1996) but, unfortunately, these are not available in English. In 1903, Ólafur Daviðsson published "Islaendische Zauberzeichen und Zauberbuecher" in German, but he based his analysis on a few, mainly late, manuscripts and did not go into any great detail regarding the operations of the Icelandic magicians.

An even greater surprise is that these preserved volumes of Icelandic sorcery have been so little exploited and largely ignored by modern practitioners of Rune magic. Instead, much emphasis is given to the characters of the various Futhark rows (Elder, Anglo-Frisian and Younger) and their esoteric interpretation, mainly based on the evidence of three Rune poems and a handful of archaeological finds whose magical significance will always remain the subject of debate. As will be seen, the use of Runic characters continued in Iceland, with explicitly magical associations, for hundreds of years after the conversion; not only that, there were many possible Rune-rows, many of which are virtually unrecognisable to those educated only in the Elder Futhark and its derivatives. On the other hand, the use of Runes plays a relatively minor part in the early modern magic of Iceland. Is it possible that we have been barking up the wrong tree all the time?

This also raises the thorny issue of semantics and terminology. What is magic? What is a grimoire? Is a book of magic necessarily a grimoire? Most importantly, is an

Icelandic book of magic by definition a book of Icelandic magic? One can agonise interminably over such definitions; indeed, some academics do so, excruciatingly so, with the net effect that the reader has to plough through their works with gritted teeth and perhaps even lays the book down in despair before coming to the main conclusions. As Richard Kieckhefer has pointed out, magic in the Middle Ages – and this applies also to the early modern period – is a kind of crossroads where different pathways in culture converge. A leechbook, or book of healing, might contain items that would be considered perfectly sensible to the average person today, such as the preparation of a soup with certain herbs to cure a stomach ache; but the same recipe might well be accompanied, as an integral part of the exercise, by the command to collect the herbs at a certain time of day or phase of the moon, and to say a prayer, charm or incantation as they are being prepared. Likewise, a curse on an enemy might contain appeals to the Christian god or commands in his name: does that make it a matter of religion rather than of magic? For the present purpose, I will therefore consider a 'magical' operation as anything that involves the use of signs, staves, incantations, charms or appeals to some unseen power to achieve an effect that could not ordinarily be achieved by physical, chemical or biological action. As regards the definition of 'book of magic', I include any volume in which a significant part is devoted to such magical operations, and I use the term 'grimoire' very loosely to describe a book of magic.

The most recent grimoire referred to in this work dates from around 1860. When referring to Iceland, terms such as 'mediaeval', 'renaissance' and 'early modern' can be deceptive because of the distinctly different level of development, as will be seen in Chapter 1. For example, in his "History of Iceland" Jón R. Hjálmarsson writes: "To give an indication of the importance of telegraphy, it has been said that only with its introduction [in 1906] did the Middle Ages finally come to an end in Iceland.[1]"

My ultimate aim, as first conceived, was extremely ambitious: to fill this gap in knowledge by producing a comprehensive survey of the techniques of Icelandic magic, based on a reading of all the extant grimoires and a thorough reading – in Icelandic – of the relevant chapters in both volumes of Jón Árnason's "Íslenzkar Þjóðsögur og Æfintýri". As my sixtieth birthday was approaching, however, I realised that I should perhaps have started on this project about forty years ago, beginning by studying Icelandic and folklore at university instead of politics. Therefore, I shall concentrate instead on what I can actually do at the present time. Given the current level of my ability in the Icelandic language, I will focus on five grimoires that have already been translated into English (referring where necessary to the original manuscript), one grimoire that I have succeeded in translating from the Icelandic, and such folk tales and legends as have already been translated into English. Given time, diligence and patience, I may yet succeed in producing a definitive work on Icelandic magic, but one has to start somewhere. A study of Icelandic magic based on thorough analysis of six original manuscripts is still a considerable

---

[1] Jón R. Hjálmarsson, "History of Iceland from the Settlement to the Present Day", 3rd edition, Reykjavík 2007, p. 128.

achievement and has – as far as I know – never been attempted before. All the illustrations of the magical signs and images have been faithfully reproduced from the originals and are not copied in my own hand. This has the advantage of avoiding transcription errors, a problem which plagued even the owners of the original books of magic.

Finally, a word of warning: this is not a book of instruction on 'how to perform Icelandic magic', and some may find it rather dry reading. However, if you are looking for a book that presents the facts, you have come to the right place.

A Note on Orthography and Pronunciation

The Icelandic alphabet contains a number of characters that are not used in English. Furthermore, the pronunciation of vowels can be considerably changed by the addition of an accent over them. Here follows a brief guide to these characters and their pronunciation.

Þ Pronounced with a hard 'th', as in 'thorn'.

Ð/ð Pronounced with a soft 'th', as in 'this'.

J/j Pronounced as 'y' in English.

G/g Pronunciation varies; usually hard (as in 'get') at the beginning of words, a 'y' sound in the middle (ægishjálmur), and 'ch' (as in 'loch') at the end.

Æ/æ Pronounced as the English word 'eye'.

ö Pronounced like the 'u' in the English word 'blur'.

a As in British English 'man'.

á As in the exclamation 'ow!'

e As in British English 'men'.

é An 'e' preceded by a 'y' sound, as in 'yes'.

i/y A short 'i', as in 'lift'.

í/ý A long 'i', as in 'bean'.

o A short 'o', as in 'cod'.

ó A long, more rounded 'o', as in 'goat'.

u A short 'u', as in 'but'.

ú A long 'u', as in 'moot'.

ei Roughly as in English 'their'.

au Does not exist in English; best reproduced by pronouncing an open 'a' (as in the exclamation 'ah'), immediately merging into a closed 'u' as in French 'tu'. Somewhat similar to Dutch 'ui' but quite different to German 'au'.

CHAPTER 1

ICELANDIC MAGIC IN CONTEXT

The present work is by no means intended as an ethnographic study, nor is it my purpose to devote any great attention to the witchcraft trials of the 16th to early 18th centuries. However, something must at least be said about the people who practised magic and took the trouble to commit some of their operations to writing, and about the world they inhabited. Only then can we fully understand the purposes and preoccupations that emerge from the grimoires.

The environment and the economy

First of all, one must consider the geographic and economic environment of Iceland in the early modern period. Life here on the very fringe of the European sphere was undoubtedly very harsh. In total area, the island is nearly four-fifths the size of England, but of this area only 23% is vegetated and able to support farming of any kind. As already mentioned in the introduction, arable land is scarce and most farming is pastoral, predominantly involving sheep. Indeed, the Icelandic word *fé* can mean either 'sheep' or 'money', depending on the context, which shows how important livestock farming was. The interior of the country is dominated by glaciers and vast, uninhabitable wastes of volcanic grit, so most of the human populace tends to hug the coastline or inhabit the grassy valleys extending inland. The bounty of the sea, in the form of fish, whales, seals and seabirds, has always been essential to economic prosperity (if one could call it prosperity in the early modern period). Driftwood from the sea was often the only source of timber for some isolated communities in this treeless environment[2]. The population, therefore, tended to live in very scattered communities – mostly isolated farmsteads – and Iceland had hardly even any villages until the 18th Century (even Reykjavík did not become a town until 1786). Roads and bridges were almost non-existent, and most travel and transport on land was done either on foot or by utilizing the sturdy Icelandic ponies, the loads being strapped onto their backs rather than hauled by cart. Astonishingly, even the wheelbarrow, a simple but highly useful tool, did not arrive in Iceland until the nineteenth century.

Throughout much of the period under consideration, the people of Iceland also had to contend with other factors that only served to increase hardship. There was the period of climatic cooling from approximately 1550 to 1850, bringing harsher winters and shorter summers. Several major volcanic eruptions occurred, culminating in the

---

[2] At the time of the first settlements, Iceland had been 24-40% forested, but injudicious use of the available timber for building and firewood and its clearance for sheep farming resulted in deforestation that continued until the mid-20th Century. See Thröstur Eysteinsson "Forestry in a treeless land", Icelandic Forest Service, Egilsstaðir, 2009.

disastrous Laki eruption of 1783-1785, reducing the human population by a quarter and bringing it to such a parlous state that the Danish government (which ruled Iceland at the time) even considered evacuating the country entirely. Nor did Iceland's relative geographic isolation give it any protection against the plagues that ravaged Europe until the mid-seventeenth century, or from the attentions of Barbary pirates. On top of all this, all trade with this, Denmark's province, was given into the hands of a select number of Danish merchants from 1602 until 1787, and the Icelanders were effectively fleeced under this monopoly. To quote Jón R. Hjálmarsson, "It has been said that of the many plagues which have afflicted the Icelanders in the course of the centuries, the Danish trade monopoly was probably the worst"[3].

Figure 1: Turf house of the type common in Iceland until the 20th Century

---

[3] Jón R. Hjálmarsson, op. cit., p.77

Law and law enforcement

Secondly, we must give attention to the system of law and its enforcement, for this also has a bearing on the purposes of the various operations detailed in the grimoires. In this respect, it is worth quoting Magnús Rafnsson at length. Although he refers specifically to the witchcraft trials of the 17th Century, his description has a bearing on the process of law in general:

> "Iceland was a rural society with no towns or villages and the local authority was the district commissioner or sheriff, who was also the local judge. These districts were around twenty in the country, each one divided into several communities or parishes. Two men were chosen to be head sheriffs or lawmen, each over one half of the country. The sheriff attended hearings each spring in the parishes where charges or suspicions of illegal activities were put to him. The sheriff could also call an assembly at other times if serious cases were brought to his attention. He acted as prosecutor and named his co-judges to decide guilt or innocence with him. If the result was a sentence of guilt, the sheriff decided the punishment. Some cases never went beyond the parish courts. The two lawmen acted as an intermediary court and could call on the law council of the parliament at Þingvellir, which by this time had lost its legislative powers. But the law council settled disputes over the law and it ratified death sentences, in some witchcraft cases after executions had taken place according to a decision by the lawmen. After 1663

all cases where guilt meant a death sentence had to be put to the law council of the general assembly."[4]

There was no constituted police force at this time or any other means for the proper detection and recording of crime. In most cases, therefore, unless sufficient evidence was present to make it worthwhile bringing a case to the attention of the sheriff, it was very much up to each individual to resolve his own problems with errant neighbours. As society was stratified, ranging from day-labourers, tenant farmers and yeomen farmers of modest means to owners of considerable estates and the Crown bailiffs, justice and the chance of a fair hearing were far from assured.

Vernacular literacy

The people of Iceland may have been poor, but for the most part they were certainly not lumpen or dull of wit. Before the adoption of Christianity, a strong tradition of orally communicated learning had existed; skaldic story-tellers from Iceland at one time held a virtual monopoly at the Norwegian royal court, and Lawmakers on the island were expected to memorise all the Commonwealth's laws by rote long before they were ever committed to parchment. Nor were they wholly unfamiliar with writing, for the runic characters were used to carve messages of a mundane nature as well as in magic, and this tradition did not die out

---

[4] Magnús Rafnsson, "Angurgapi. The Witch-hunts in Iceland", Strandagaldur, Hólmavík 2003, p.17.

completely. With the coming of Christianity, however, there came a new emphasis on the written word, the use of the Roman alphabet, and writing on parchment rather than carving on wood, bone or stone. This made it easier to commit much lengthier passages to writing, initially in Latin in the scriptoria of monasteries, but to an increasing extent in the vernacular language. At first, only the wealthier chieftains could afford to send their sons for an ecclesiastical education, but there must have been a 'trickle-down' effect into society at large for, as Gisli Sigurðsson writes:

> "Manuscripts were read out loud in the Middle Ages, and as book ownership became more common in later centuries this custom continued, even after printing had begun. In his description of Iceland from 1590, Oddur Einarsson says that farmers in Iceland entertained and delighted their guests by reading for them for hours from the sagas. In the eighteenth century it was still the main form of leisure in the evenings to read the old Icelandic sagas and recite ballads, a custom which continued into the twentieth century. It was more common for women than men to tell stories – adventures, ghost stories, stories of hidden people, or 'stories of all things, dead and alive, between heaven and earth', as Ingibjörg Lárusdóttir (1869-1949) described the subjects told by an old woman from the Húnavatn district in the northwest. People also retold printed stories, Icelandic and foreign, and itinerant travellers could find work at farms as storytellers.[5]"

---

[5] Gisli Sigurðsson, "Oral sagas, poems and lore" in "The Manuscripts of Iceland", Reykjavík 2004, pp. 8-9.

Religion and attitudes to magic

By general consensus (though, it must be said, under considerable pressure from the King of Norway, Olaf Tryggvason), Iceland had adopted Christianity at the Althing of the year 1000. Over the ensuing centuries, various proscriptive acts of the Roman Catholic Church had sought to extirpate all traces of the old religion. At first, adherents of the old gods were allowed to worship them in private, but already by 1121 the ascetic Bishop Jón Ögmundsson of Hólar had decreed that even the names of the week days were to be changed: Týr's day became 'third day', Odin's day became 'mid-week day', Thor's day became 'fifth day' and Freya's day became 'fast day'. Loður's day[6] (Saturday) became 'bath day', while the sun and moon were considered sufficiently part of the Christian god's creation to retain their respective days. As will be shown, the attempt to eliminate every facet of belief in the gods of the old religion was not entirely successful, for appeals to them still crop up in the grimoires of the seventeenth century and beyond, but it is very doubtful whether any organised cult of Odin still existed by this time[7]. The Roman Catholic period lasted until 1550, when the Lutheran faith was imposed by the Danish king and native Icelandic converts after a series of bloody

---

[6] The etymology of the sixth day of the week in this and other Nordic countries is a moot point. It may be derived from Loður (a brother of Odin) or from Lóki (which I consider unlikely), or it may be that it was always 'bath day', this being the day when people took a full bath.

[7] The persistence of belief in the old gods, the Æsir and Vanir, in the centuries following the conversion to Christianity is a subject which still has to be fully explored.

confrontations culminating in the execution of the last Catholic bishop, Jón Árason.

Even in the Icelandic law book of 1281, "sorcery, soothsaying, waking up trolls, and heathen practices"[8] were included with murder in the list of capital offences, but sorcery and witchcraft do not appear to have been persecuted with any great vigour in the Catholic period. There was only one burning, of a sister in a convent, and this was for blasphemy rather than witchcraft. According to Magnús Rafnsson[9], "There are hardly any indications that the Catholic Church actively tried to wipe out belief in the occult. Part of the explanation for this tolerance could be that many of the things that later generations regarded as superstitious magic are not that different from the prayers and healing practices of medieval times." Things were to change radically, however, after the conversion to Lutheranism, and a new intolerance took hold. Any discovered act of magic was vigorously prosecuted, whether committed with evil or benign intent, and even the possession of a few magical staves on paper or on an object could be enough to see a person condemned. The Icelandic witch trials lasted from 1554 (just four years after the conversion) until 1719 and are roughly coterminous with the

---

[8] 'Angurgapi', p.26. It should be mentioned that state authorities have never been officially tolerant of magical practices by lay persons. Richard Kieckhefer states that "in a single year, the emperor Augustus (63 BC – AD 14) is said to have had two thousand magical scrolls burned." (R. Kieckhefer, "Magic in the Middle Ages", Canto Edition, Cambridge University Press, Cambridge 2000.)

[9] 'Angurgapi', p.11.

witch craze that prevailed throughout Europe (especially in the Protestant countries) at this time.

The trial records reveal significant differences from the prosecutions in Europe and open up important insights into the idiosyncratic nature of magical practice in Iceland. Firstly, "the diabolism that played such a large part in the accusations in Europe is not found in the Icelandic court cases. Though Halldór Finnbogason was burnt in 1685 for reciting 'Our father who art in Hell...' etc., his crime was blasphemy and witchcraft is not mentioned in the records[10]". This stands in contrast to the accusations in other countries, where the emphasis was frequently on pacts with the devil and nocturnal flights to some secret place to hold diabolic Sabbaths. Another factor is the inversion of the ratio of females to males who were accused and sentenced. In Denmark (Iceland's ruler at this time), about one thousand persons were burned at the stake and 95% of these were female; in Iceland, 21 people were burned (out of about 134 brought to trial) and, of these, only one was a woman. The third factor – and the most salient for the purpose of this study – is that a third of the cases involved the possession and use of magical staves or signs. As Owen Davies has written in his book "Grimoires. A History of Magic Books":

> "The *one place* in Europe where grimoires did feature prominently in the witch trials was Iceland. Around 134 trials are known to have occurred in this former Danish territory, and nearly a third of

---

[10] 'Angurgapi' p.15

these involved grimoires, written spells, or runes and symbols derived from them.[11]" [My italics.]

Regrettably, for the modern historian, part of the punishment of accused sorcerers frequently involved having their books of magic burned in front of their noses. Many other owners of grimoires will no doubt have disposed of them quietly rather than be caught in their possession.

As to the type of people who practised magic (or were at least accused of it) in Iceland during the witch trials, they seem to have come from all levels of society, although those who had power and influence were often able to avoid an unfavourable verdict or, if sentenced, to get off with a lighter punishment.

Conclusion

The picture that emerges is of life in a largely subsistence economy of fishing and pastoral farming, where famine could be just around the corner. It was vital to ensure a good catch of fish, to mow hay quickly while the weather was good, or to guard one's flocks against dangers of all kinds. The rule of law was valued – as it had been since the time of the Icelandic Republic – but its administration depended on infrequent visits from what were effectively circuit judges, and the verdicts of the latter could be influenced by the power and standing of the respective

---

[11] Owen Davies "Grimoires. A History of Magic Books", OUP, Oxford 2009, p. 71.

parties. Individuals (particularly those who were poor and lacking influence) were therefore dependent on their own resources when it came to finding justice. External trade was regulated in a way that worked to the disadvantage of Icelanders. Religion was in a state of flux throughout the period, with memories of the old, heathen religion and practices preserved in stories, folk customs and superstitions even as the new, Lutheran faith supplanted Roman Catholicism. Little wonder, then, that people turned to magic in order to gain some semblance of control over their precarious existences, and that they recorded some details of their magical workings and the associated staves and signs in handwritten, parchment books.

CHAPTER 2

THE BOOKS OF MAGIC

A number of magical scripts from Iceland have been preserved in various libraries and archives. They vary greatly in size and format, and also in state of preservation, some being much damaged or barely legible. The modern researcher is fortunate in being able to refer to an online catalogue[12] encompassing the manuscript collections of the Icelandic National Library, the Árni Magnússon Institute for Icelandic Studies (both in Reykjavík) and the Arnamagnæan Institute in Copenhagen. Manuscripts are being added to this catalogue all the time, and digital images of some of them are even available to inspect and to download as PDF files. For my present purposes, I have concentrated on five manuscripts that have already been translated into English, plus one that I have translated from Icelandic into English. In order to avoid confusion and facilitate referencing by other scholars, I will refer to them by their respective shelfmarks together with (where appropriate) a secondary title, as listed in the library catalogues.

---

[12] www.handrit.is

AM 434 a 12mo 'Lækningakver' (ca 1500)

Figure 2: Sample of AM 424 a 12mo

This fairly small (10.4 x 7.7 cm / 4 x 3 inches) book is held in the Arnamagnæan Institute in Copenhagen. It contains 40 leaves. It has been translated into English, with comments, by Ben Waggoner[13]. Waggoner has used an earlier translation into Danish, "Den islandske lægebog" by Kristian Kålund (1907), as his source. The manuscript is in the handwriting of two different scribes, but the authors are

---

[13] Ben Waggoner "Norse Magical and Herbal Healing", The Troth, New Haven (Connecticut) 2011.

unknown. The bulk of the text is a leech-book of healing in the time when magic often formed an integral part of the healer's practices and the modern distinction between 'natural' and 'supernatural' means and methods had not yet been made[14]. It can, therefore, be difficult to decide which sections of it can be considered magical operations and which ones are recognisable as early attempts at a 'scientific' approach. However, some of the operations in the book – especially those that do not relate to healing - have an undeniably magical content and will be taken into account. Apart from the healing work that is purely of a practical nature and the lists of favourable and unfavourable times, there are 27 workings that can be denoted as magical spells[15].

---

[14] For more on the subject of mediaeval attitudes to magic, read Richard Kieckhefer's "Magic in the Middle Ages", Canto Edition, Cambridge University Press, Cambridge 2000.
[15] For the sake of brevity, the term 'spell' will be used henceforth to describe any magical operation.

ATA, Amb 2, F 16:26 'Isländska Svartkonstboken (Book of magic)' (1550-1650?)

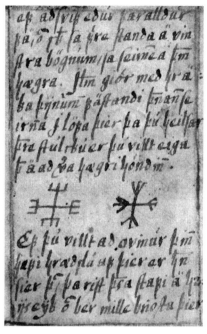

Figure 3: Sample of the Stockholm MS

This is certainly the most famous of the Icelandic magical manuscripts, owing to its translation into English and publication by Dr Stephen E. Flowers under the title of "The Galdrabók"[16]. Because all the volumes discussed in this work can be designated as a *galdrabók* (pl. *galdrabækur*), or book of magic, and because the Swedish shelfmark is even more unwieldy than the Icelandic ones, I will use the

---

[16] Stephen E. Flowers, Ph.D., "The Galdrabók", 2nd revised edition, Runa-Raven Press, Smithville (TX) 2005.

designation 'Stockholm MS' throughout this work[17]. This grimoire is written in four separate hands. It was initially begun by an unknown Icelander in the latter half of the 16th Century and subsequently added to by another Icelander, also in the late 16th Century. Yet another Icelander added more spells, the style of handwriting indicating that this was done in the 17th Century. The book was at some point taken to Denmark, where a Dane added the last four of the 47 spells. Flowers writes that "This Dane must also have had the use of other Icelandic books of magic, now lost, from which he collected these spells.[18]" He continues "In 1682 the book was acquired by the Danish philologist J.G. Sparfvenfelt and was later acquired by the Swedes for their growing collection of 'Gothic' monuments and manuscripts. Eventually it found its way into the Academy of Sciences (State Historical Museum) in Stockholm, where it is now." The Stockholm MS therefore spans nearly one hundred years. In 1921 it was translated into Swedish by Natan Lindqvist and published under the title "En islänsk Svartkonstbok från 1500-talet". As the Stockholm archive does not list its collection on the internet as thoroughly as the Icelandic National Library, I have been unable to establish its size and format. However, I have a digitized copy of the manuscript in my collection.

---

[17] My reference for the shelfmark is in a paper by Prof. Stephen A. Mitchell, "Leechbooks, Manuals, and Grimoires. On the early History of Magical Texts in Scandinavia" available on academia.edu.

[18] Flowers, op. cit., p.18.

Lbs 143 8vo 'Galdrakver' (ca 1670)

Figure 4: Sample of Lbs 143 8vo

This fairly well-preserved manuscript residing in the Icelandic National and University Library consists of 27 leaves of parchment measuring 12.8 x 7.8 cm (approx. 5 x 3 inches), contained in a leather wallet. It is written in a single hand. The original scribe is unknown, but it eventually came into the keeping of Bishop Hannes Finnsson (1739-1796) of Skálholt. This book of magic is interesting in that it was produced at the height of the Icelandic witchcraft persecution; it probably survived because it contains mainly apotropaic spells and talismans, the one curse in it being the

109th Psalm! As well as prayers and talismans, it contains a number of typically Icelandic staves and signs. In all, it covers 20 distinct magical intentions. We are fortunate in that this volume was published by the Icelandic National Library in 2004 as a delightful, two-volume set; the first volume is a facsimile of the manuscript, while the second volume gives a letter-for-letter transcription, a version in modern Icelandic spelling, and translations into Danish, English and German by native speakers of those languages.

Lbs 2413 8vo 'Rúna- og galdrakver' (ca 1800)

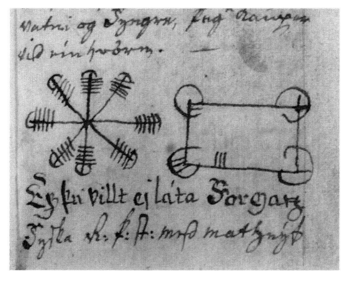

Figure 5: Sample of Lbs 2413 8vo

In his book "Tvær Galdraskræður" (2008)[19], Magnús Rafnsson describes this as "the largest collection of magical staves in a single manuscript even when compared to those collected by amateur scholars almost a century later." The manuscript measures 10 x 8 cm (approx. 4 x 3 inches) and has 74 leaves. Nothing is known of its history or how the library acquired it. At the time of writing, it had not been digitized, nor even listed in the online archive but, thanks to the patient efforts of Alaric Hall, I was able to view each page in individual photographs.. Furthermore, it is one of the two volumes translated into English, complete with accurate renderings of the magic staves, in "Tvær

---

[19] Magnús Rafnsson, "Tvær Galdraskræður. Two Icelandic Books of Magic", Strandagaldur, Hólmavík 2008.

Galdraskræður". It is listed in the 1918 edition of the library's catalogue as being written in one hand. For the most part, the writing is cursive and of the type one might expect around 1800, but in many instances the writer has clearly made an effort to reproduce a much older kind of script that was current in the 17th Century. One may draw the conclusion that the writer had access to older manuscripts and copied from them. This manuscript, which contains no less than 187 magical spells of various kinds (though the intentions are frequently duplicated), was the subject of my previous publication on the subject of Icelandic magic[20].

---

[20] Christopher A. Smith "The Icelandic Tradition of Magic: Analysis of a Late Eighteenth-Century Icelandic Galdrabók", published in "Occult Traditions", Numen Books 2011.

Lbs 764 8vo (ca 1820)

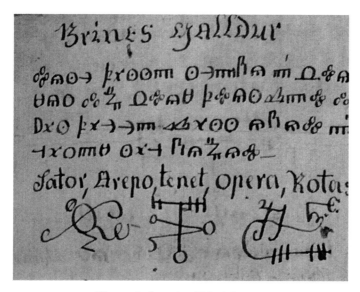

Figure 6: Sample of Lbs 764 8vo

This grimoire is the second of the two books described and translated in "Tvær Galdraskræður". Like Lbs 2413 8vo, it was not listed at handrit.is but I have confirmed its availability in the manuscripts collection of the Icelandic National Library and viewed photographs of all its pages. As usual, the scribe is unknown. It measures 14 x 8.5 cm (approx. 5.5 x 3.3 inches) and comprises only 14 leaves wrapped in a leather wallet. The first half of the spells contained in it appear to be of European origin, consisting of protective signs and texts in Latin. Among the Latin texts is the Lord's Prayer backwards, the only such example in

Icelandic grimoires, according to Magnús Rafnsson[21]. The second part is a collection of the 'traditional' type of staves and texts, but the texts are written with a secret alphabet, which Magnús appears to have deciphered (no key to it is given in the manuscript). In all, it contains 51 items, although the purpose of many of the signs in the first part is unspecified.

-----

[21] This is not absolutely correct: spell number 45 in the Stockholm MS also calls for the Lord's Prayer to be said backwards.

ÍB 383 4to 'Huld' (ca 1860)

Figure 7: Sample of 'Huld' Manuscript

This manuscript is of a relatively late date and is the only one among the six considered here to be attributed to a named individual, Geir Vigfússon (1813-1880) of Akureyri, whose occupation is described as 'scholar'. The same man has a number of works attributed to him in the library's manuscript collection, and it is safe to assume that he was an antiquarian. The Huld MS consists of 27 leaves plus end boards and measures 22 x 27 cm (approx. 8.7 x 10.6 inches). Digitized images of the manuscript are available to view and download at handrit.is. The manuscript is written in a fine hand and the script is often beautifully decorated. The first part consists of carefully composed tables of runic characters, secret alphabets and numerical and alphabetic ciphers. The second part is a numbered collection of magical staves –

thirty in all - and their purposes, the text frequently including runes and ciphers. The runes that are used are from a later Icelandic row that is not entirely given in any of the tables in the first part, and the ciphers in Roman characters are sometimes inconsistent, but by a process of deduction I was able to interpret them with a little help from my Icelandic friends. It may be assumed that Geir Vigfússon had access to one or more older grimoires and copied them into this volume.

A translation into English of the Huld MS, by Justin Foster, has become available since the initial draft of this book was completed. It can be found online at www.academia.edu. (See bibliography).

CHAPTER 3

PURPOSES AND PREOCCUPATIONS

Before moving to the main body of this book – a discussion of the techniques of Icelandic magic – it is necessary to consider the intentions with which magic was used within the context outlined in Chapter 1. Such analysis is helpful in many ways. Firstly, it helps to explain people's moral motivations and whether they adopted a relatively passive or, conversely, an active stance towards perceived threats and grievances. Secondly, it acquaints us with the practical aspects of life that were important to them as they eked out a living in a harsh natural environment and a society where justice was far from assured. Finally, it gives us a glimpse, through their eyes, of the supernatural world as it was perceived at that time.

The question of 'white' and 'black' magic

Even in today's secular and materialistic society (or perhaps in revolt against it), magic and the supernatural continue to exercise a fascination, as witnessed by television programmes such as 'Charmed' and 'Buffy the Vampire Slayer', and by the burgeoning fantasy genre of fiction. There is also a lingering fear of it in the popular mind, and the figure of the 'wicked witch' or the 'evil sorcerer' is perpetuated in books, pantomime and cinema. We have to ask how much of a reality it was for Icelanders in centuries past and to what extent magic was used for nefarious purposes. The tricky issue here is value judgement: are we to judge the intentions expressed in these grimoires by modern standards or by the standards of the seventeenth century? And if we are to attempt to judge them by the latter standards, through whose eyes in particular? As already stated, sorcery, soothsaying, waking up trolls, and heathen practices were already proscribed by the laws of 1281, but the Roman Catholic Church did remarkably little to eradicate them in practice. It was only with new and more puritanical attitudes after the Reformation that the witch hunts began, and then any use of magic, with whatever intention, could be enough to get a person outlawed, flogged or even burned alive. For the purpose of the present work, I have adopted a pragmatic approach. If the intention of a magical act is to help or protect a human being, without harming another person, or only to send back harmful magic that another has sent, it is deemed to be of benign intent. Those intended to operate within the sphere of normal animal husbandry are also deemed to be benign, as are operations designed to discover or catch thieves. Magical intentions that are expressly intended to harm people or livestock, or to restrict the free will of humans, are regarded as malign. Borderline cases and those where the intention is obscure or unspecified are designated as neutral. Of course, there will always be 'grey' areas. For example, I have categorised spells to soothe anger as 'benign', spells to change someone else's disposition (in the magician's favour) as 'neutral', and spells intended to gain the love of a girl or woman as 'malign', though all of them interfere with free will. It is impossible to escape value judgement, so to avoid becoming mired in a philosophical debate I must emphasise that the judgement is entirely my own. It must also be said that six books of magic constitute a very small sample from which to work and, even within this sample, many intentions are duplicated or even repeated several times. Statistical analysis is a famously imperfect tool, but it must nevertheless be applied – within its limits – if we are to make some sense of the material.

Based on these criteria, a thorough analysis of the 383 intentions and subordinate intentions listed in the six grimoires shows that more than half of them are of benign intent, and nearly half of these are intended purely to protect in some way, sometimes against a single event or situation but most often to provide lasting protection. The next largest category consists of the 'neutral' intentions that are neither expressly benign nor expressly malign. These number 106, and include spells designed to gain an advantage in a situation without deliberately and knowingly harming another person or his property. Only 77 spells – about 20% - can be said to be definitely malign and intended to harm people or property, or to make people act in a way that is not in their own interest. To those seeking for a 'colour code', it would appear at first sight that the picture is approximately 50% white, 20% black and 30% 'grey'. However, every picture includes shadow as well as light, and it is important to read both. The full conclusion will have to wait until the end of the chapter, after we have examined what the benign workings were used for.

Apotropaic magic

By far the biggest single category among the magical workings seen in the grimoires is that of intentions designed to ward off evil or harm of some kind. These take various forms, but talismans tend to predominate. Many are against 'evil' or 'harm' of an unspecified nature, but we may assume that these include protection against magic or other supernatural agencies. Some of them, sixteen in all, are explicitly intended to avert the effects of magic. A fairly typical one is contained in Lbs 2413 8vo: "*Við heitingum ber á þér þetta innsigli á helguðum pappir á brjósti*" (Against imprecations, carry this sigil on sanctified paper on your breast).

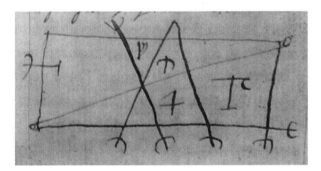

Figure 8: Item 144 in Lbs 2413 8vo

Another, from the older Lbs 143 8vo 'Galdrakver', reads "*Þessir fjórir eftir fylgjandi stafir standa við öllum galdri úr fjórum áttum veraldarinnar, og ber þá á þér*" (These four symbols guard against all magic from all four directions of the world, and bear them on thee).

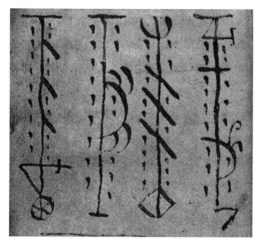

Figure 9: Item 9 in Lbs 143 8vo

As already stated, talismans tend to predominate, but against immediate danger from magic one might also trace a certain sign on one's forehead, while fasting, using saliva and the leech (ring) finger of the left hand. Prayers, incantations and washing rituals were also used. As we shall see, apotropaic signs were also used to protect livestock against magic or to cure them of its effects.

As well as evil magic, supernatural entities such as ghosts and evil spirits were a major concern. Most people in the modern, English-speaking world tend to think of ghosts as flitting, insubstantial beings that can pass through walls and inflict only psychological harm by the terror they instil. The word is actually quite inappropriate as a translation of the Icelandic concept. The *draugur*, as described in the sagas and the folk-tales, is more like an animated corpse, often with great strength, that can physically attack living humans. It can be raised from the grave by a magician and sent to do harm. Magicians were also believed to be able to create or summon other entities and send them to harm or kill. Such ghosts and evil spirits on a wrathful errand are collectively known as 'sendings'. At least ten of the operations in the six books of magic reviewed relate to ghosts and evil spirits, and three are designed to return a *sending* to its sender. One of them, an incantation with the title '*Ein stefna*' (A summons) from Lbs 2413 8vo, is worth quoting in full with the relevant wording in bold for emphasis:

"To order away a ghost[22] or an evil spirit[23] when seeing it or knowing it is near oneself or others. I take as my witness the powerful Trinity of God and the wounds of Jesus Christ against those that wish my damnation, **or with sorcery will send me** cruel devils[24]. May my summons stand as on a pillar of steel to the perfect blindness of my enemies, to be their curse and to the condemnation, decay and rotting of the Devil himself. **He who has sent me a revenant, a terrible evil, a ghost or a devil**, may he go cursing into a burning hell. If an imp of the Devil wants to come near to me I summon you with strong words down into the lowest hell so that you will forever burn there. May the heavens hate you, the sun scare you, God's angels pursue you so you will fall screaming into hell's ice and cruel nails will pierce you as Jael killed Sisera. But if you linger a moment longer I summon you a second time by the blessed victory signs of Sebaoth that you will sink into the lowest hell **or he who has sent you**. Sink

---

[22] *Draug*

[23] *vondum anda*

[24] *eða með galdri grimma djöfla senda*

there as of old Cori, Datan and Abicam. **All these wishes work on you unless you meet him who has sent you**. Grab him, you cursed one, screaming in anger so he will be torn apart, his flesh crushed, his soul be terrified, so his understanding will all be in tatters. Torment his soul and flesh so you will yourself be less tormented come doomsday. **If you are sent to me again** and want to bother me or harm me, I will summon you.[25]"

Yet other apotropaic workings relate to ogres, trolls and elves, but these are few. One in AM 434 a 12mo is 'against troll-riding' and appears to be a short prayer of exorcism to expel "ogres and ogresses, trolls and evil beings". There are two items in the Stockholm MS 'against troll-shot', but these are identical; it may be that the scribe forgot that he had already recorded the working. Only one spell (also in AM 434 a 12mo) is against 'hardship caused by elves'.

A significant number of spells are intended to protect against attack or visits by human enemies or 'evil men'. In these there is no explicit mention of malignant magic, and they appear to refer to physical confrontations. Finally, one talismanic spell is claimed to protect a house against fire as well as visitations by wicked men.

[25] Translation by Magnús Rafnsson with my own minor orthographic emendations.

Farming, fishing and trade

Farming, fishing and trade have always been the mainstays of Iceland's economy, and remain so even today. It therefore comes as little surprise that a high proportion of the spells in the books of magic centre on these activities. Just over half of the workings in this category relate to healing domestic animals, curing them of the effects of evil magic, protecting them (sometimes against magic) or controlling them. There are also spells designed to catch livestock thieves and others to harm livestock, so this category overlaps to some extent with those of 'crime and disputes' and 'malignant magic'.

Figure 10: "When livestock has been injured by an evil spell, this symbol shall be made in its own blood, whether ram or bull, on the beast itself, and it will recover." (From Lbs 143 8vo)

What is perhaps surprising, given the perils of sea and weather, is that relatively few spells relate to fishing and all of these are in Lbs 2413 8vo. Four of them, for successful fishing, involve carving a stave on the boat or on the sinker, a fifth uses the SATOR rebus to release tackle when it is stuck on the sea bottom, and a sixth is for good progress when rowing.

Gaining an advantage when trading, or at least getting a fair deal and seeing to it that the other party kept the bargain, was the aim of eight spells. To these may be speculatively added a ninth, contained in AM 434 a 12mo: *"Against tricks: sans, gante, gantes, gantisim, gantissimus."*

Towards the end of summer, reaping and mowing also had to be done to provide grain for bread and winter hay for livestock. Because of the capricious Icelandic weather, it was essential to get on with the job as quickly as possible when the crops were dry. Scythes have to be sharpened frequently and well using a whetstone. Three spells are mentioned, in three separate books of magic, with the aim of enhancing the efficiency of the whetstone.

Friendship, favour and influence

Among the 'benign' and 'neutral' spells, a very large category is made up of operations designed to change how others are disposed towards the magician. The famous Ægishjálmur (Helm of Awe, or of Ægir) symbol and its associated rituals fall into this category, but there are many more with a similar intent that do not involve this stave. In general terms, they involve workings to avert the anger and hostility of others, to sway one's fellow men towards a more favourable disposition, to acquire friendship, to get requests granted or to gain ubiquitous love and popularity. In all, no less than 34 of the listed spells are devoted to these ends, not including the darker spells to instil fear which I have categorised under 'malign magic'. They also display great variation with regards to the general methods by which they are accomplished, such as contact, proximity, talismans and washing rituals.

Crime and disputes

If the number of magical spells is anything to go by, theft must have been a major preoccupation for Icelanders. Five are devoted to preventing theft, three to summoning or trapping the thief, two to compelling him (or her) to return the stolen goods, and no less than 23 to discovering who has stolen goods, mainly by some type of divination. There are even two spells, in different books, to make someone become a thief. Indeed, the only one of these magic books that has nothing at all to say on the subject of theft is Lbs 143 8vo 'Galdrakver' (1670). When one adds to these the workings that are probably nefarious, such as inducing a charmed sleep, making oneself invisible or breaking a lock, one gets the impression of a society in the grip of kleptomania. This was probably not the case; the fear of theft may have outweighed its prevalence in a society where people had few possessions and the few they had were essential to their survival. A study of criminality in early modern Iceland is beyond the scope of this work, but I hope to return to the matter at some future date.

Another eight spells are intended to ensure that the user wins disputes or lawsuits, or at least reach a settlement.

Healing

In an age when trained doctors were virtually unheard of, the healing of sickness and injuries was naturally an important concern at all levels of society. Indeed, the earliest book of magic consulted in this work, 'Lækningakver' (Book of Healing), is mostly devoted to this subject and magic simply forms – for the most part – an element of its administration. Nineteen healing spells are mentioned in all, not counting those purely for the healing of livestock, and of these nine are from 'Lækningakver'[26]. There are spells to cure physical ailments such as headaches, colic, seasickness, swelling and inflammation, pain in the eyes and boils. Four spells are to stem the flow of blood, and three are intended to help in childbirth. Five are directed at cures of a more psychological nature such as weeping, melancholy, insomnia and madness 'sent upon one by another'.

Love and seduction

Spells to gain the erotic love of another are perennial and ubiquitous. Because they interfere with the free will of another person, I consider them 'malignant' rather than 'benign' or 'neutral', but they are so numerous that they deserve a category of their own. All of them are directed towards forcing a female to love the user of the spell; none have the aim of gaining the erotic love of a man. It is tempting to conclude that amorous magic was exclusively a male concern in Iceland, but the data sources from which we are working here are limited. The vast majority of spells of this type occur in Lbs 2413 8vo, and this may skew the statistics. Most of the spells use the Icelandic word *stúlka*

---

[26] AM 434 a 12mo 'Lækningakver' contains much more on healing, but not all of its items can be considered magical.

(girl), but three use the word *kona* (woman). Two of them promise all kinds of suffering unless the girl or woman complies, and in this sense they are very similar to the threat issued by Skírnir to Gerð in *Skírnismál*. Another, "That no-one corrupts the girl you desire", can also be added in this category of sexual covetousness. Other spells pertaining to human sexual relations include one to make a girl pregnant and two that are tests of virginity. It should be noted that in the first trial for witchcraft after the Reformation, the priest Oddur Þorsteinsson was accused of seducing and raping his sister-in-law with the aid of magic and sorcery in accordance with the grimoires found in his possession[27].

Divination

The topic of divination has already been touched upon under 'Crime and disputes'. When the operations with the purpose of identifying a thief are added to divinatory operations of a general nature, these add up to a significant number. The techniques will be discussed in detail, but for now it can be said that only three are mentioned for certain: oneiromancy, bibliomancy and scrying. There is one possible instance of necromancy.

---

[27] Oddur was found guilty and sentenced to pay compensation for the rape or lose both his ears. The use of sorcery and possession of grimoires brought an additional sentence of being outlawed from the whole of northern Iceland and losing his right hand, unless the Danish authorities decided to show leniency. The King's representatives showed leniency and, with help from relatives, he paid the compensation, so he kept his hand and his ears. Thirty years later, this same person became a priest in Strandir and served well into the seventeenth century (see *Angurgapi*, p. 23).

Games and sports

A small but still significant category of spells is devoted to success in playing cards or dice and in wrestling.

Luck and wishes

Sixteen spells can be identified that have the general purpose of bringing luck or getting one's wish. Most of these involve the making and carrying of a talisman.

Spells of purely malign intent

Excluding the 'love' (read 'seduction') spells already mentioned, there are no less than fifty-seven malign spells expressly intended to bring harm, misery or even death to an enemy. The largest sub-categories are spells to instil fear, to harm livestock, and to make someone fall into a charmed sleep from which they cannot be roused[28]. Other specific intentions include making a person lose their way (presumably in a fog or blizzard), raising a northern blizzard, making someone become a thief, preventing someone from fishing, inflicting intolerable farting and causing someone to die by falling off his horse. The methods by which they are achieved vary greatly. The nastiest imprecation, a wide-ranging curse, is drawn straight from the Bible – the 109th Psalm!

This covers the main categories, but the list of intentions is not exhaustive. As the reader will have discerned, there are big areas of overlap, for example between the categories

---

[28] I note that only one of the 'sleep' spells includes an antidote.

of 'divination' and 'crime and disputes'. My purpose here is simply to give a foretaste of what is to come and to discern the main preoccupations for which Icelanders resorted to magic in the early modern period.

Conclusions

Taken together, the large categories of apotropaic magic and spells of purely malign intent indicate a widespread fear of evil magic and the fact that this fear may have been justified. If the ratio of defensive workings to aggressive workings is any indicator, people mainly saw themselves as the victims rather than the perpetrators. There appears to have been a great fear of ghosts – or rather reanimated corpses – and evil spirits, both of which could be raised by a magician and sent against an enemy. The paucity of spells against trolls and elves shows that these wights were not a major concern.

Magic could be used to get one's way in a wide variety of everyday issues, such as healing, winning over a prospective sexual partner or protecting livestock. In an uncertain world, divination and general 'luck' magic were used to stave off the unforeseen. Reputation and one's esteem among fellow men apparently formed an important preoccupation, and that can be understood in a society where the individual was very dependent on the goodwill of others for survival. When things went wrong in this respect, when thefts occurred or disputes broke out, magic could also be used to discover the thief or to get the better in the settlement of a lawsuit.

Except for names mentioned in the court cases and the folk tales, we do not know who the magicians were; the evidence from those sources and the preoccupations in the Icelandic grimoires would lead one to the conclusion that magic was almost entirely a male business. Of course, it may have been that women had their own magical devices and were savvy enough to keep them from the attention of the witch-finders and society at large, but we must go by the evidence that we have.

CHAPTER 4

THE MAIN TECHNIQUES OF ICELANDIC MAGIC

In the preamble to his translation of the Stockholm MS, Dr Stephen E. Flowers identifies a number of salient features that distinguish Icelandic magic from the formal procedures of the 'Western' or 'Mediterranean' tradition[29]. Many of his observations will be confirmed here, but also considerably expanded upon because we are dealing with six magical books rather than just one. It must also be said that the distinction between magic as practised in early modern Iceland and in mainland Europe (in which I count the British Isles) becomes less clear when it is remembered that Mediterranean-tradition magic was practised by a small, educated élite, while the less elaborate procedures of folk magic saw more use among the common people. In "Magic in the Middle Ages", Richard Kieckhefer leans largely upon two very different case studies, both from the 15th Century: the 'Wolfsthurn book', which is a general household manual containing items of folk magic, and the 'Munich handbook',

---

[29] Flowers, op. cit., Chapter 6 "Theory and Practice of Magic in the Galdrabók".

which involves straightforward demonic magic [30] . The procedures in the former are generally notable for their simplicity, and more closely resemble magic as practised in Iceland, while those in the latter are often quite complex and have much less in common with the Icelandic tradition. In a later study, I also hope to compare and contrast Icelandic magic with the witchcraft traditions of England and Pennsylvanian Pow-wow magic; we may then find a greater commonality.

The question of complexity is a difficult one, and we will return to this in due course. It should never be imagined that any grimoire contains everything involved in the performance of its listed spells. When reading them, it is wise to consider one's own notebooks, jottings and address books: we record only the key information that we might otherwise forget, and a single, scribbled line is often intended to lead to a process of thought and memory that will evoke all the other necessary details. In that sense, we should view these magical books as the random notes of forgotten cooks rather than the published works of leading chefs. Nevertheless, by inference and diligent study, we may be able to piece together the significant actions and ingredients of Icelandic magic.

The primacy of the magical sign as a vehicle of the intent

One of the first things to strike one, even when casually browsing the Icelandic books of magic, is the dominant

---

[30] Kieckhefer, op.cit., p.2 ff. "Two Case Studies".

position held by magical staves and images (*galdrastafir* and *galdramyndir*). Five in every six of the spells examined here have some kind of sign associated with them, and a stave may be implied even when it is not actually depicted, as in washing rituals which include the phrase "I bear the *Helm of Awe* between my brows". The staves and images vary enormously in complexity, from simple crosses with arms terminating in tridents or circles to highly elaborate combinations of lines, rectangles, circles, secondary glyphs and names of power. Whether simple or complex, they form an indispensable part of the working and are often the main or sole vehicle. A typical example of such a spell is number 123 in Lbs 2413 8vo:

> "To ensure that nobody can leave a house, no matter how many they may be, carve this stave on the threshold."

Figure 11: Item 123 in Lbs 2413 8vo

Of course, there is frequently some overlap; the magical signs may be accompanied by appeals, however vague, to a supernatural entity such as Christ, Satan or the gods of the old Nordic pantheon, but in the great majority of cases (224 out of about 360) the sign alone is considered to be sufficient. Staves are sometimes used singly and sometimes in combinations of two or more. Some spells explicitly give alternative staves for the same magical intention, while at other times the same stave is used in separate spells for completely different intentions. Occasionally, the same intention is given in different spells and books, but using different staves and somewhat different associated methods. Take, for example, the *fretrúnir* or fart-rune spells that can be found in Lbs 2413 8vo and the Stockholm MS: they all employ different signs and characters, though the intention is the same – to inflict incessant and intolerable farting on someone.

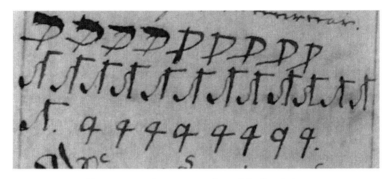

Figure 12a: 'Fart runes' from Lbs 2413 8vo

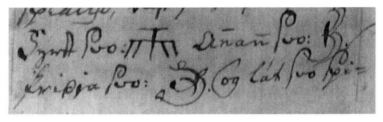

Different 'fart rune' from Lbs 2413 8vo

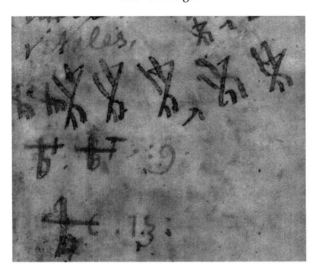

Figure 12c: 'Fart runes' from the Stockholm MS

This factor, the pre-eminence of the magical sign, is extremely characteristic of Icelandic magic, and it shows that great importance was attached to the efficacy of such signs as a means of channelling, augmenting and directing the will of the sorcerer by virtue of some inherent power of their own. In this sense, they operate very much as the runes did in the sagas about the Viking age, but whether the magical signs of the early modern period are derived from the Futhark runes is a question we must explore in a later chapter. As will be seen, the staves could be cut, shaved, burned or written onto a variety of surfaces with various instruments, but the verb most commonly used is *að rista* – to carve – even when literal carving is not meant. This is the same verb that was usually used in association with the runes, and indicates that the magical signs originate from a period when wood, stone or bone were used rather than vellum or paper. It may also be that the forceful act of carving was thought to be more potent than merely drawing the sign on a surface. However, the 'Helm of Awe' washing rituals give a clue that it could sometimes be enough simply to hold the image in one's mind.

Appeals to supernatural entities

In order to identify the workings that make no appeal at all to any kind of supernatural entity (the majority, as mentioned above), I discounted all that included any reference, however small, insignificant or suspect, to a higher power. This covered everything from mentions in prayers or incantations, the use of Judeo-Christian divine names in magical images, appeals to Satan and Beelzebub, and calls to the old, pre-Christian gods, to fragments of 'dog Latin' that might be construed as mumbled imitations of Catholic liturgy. Now we must return to these previously excluded references in order to ascertain their nature and importance, because they are still sufficiently numerous to constitute a noticeable element of magic as practised in Iceland.

Most of the references (106) are purely Judeo-Christian in origin, and a high proportion of these consist of seals, or *sigilli*. The Seal of Solomon is a favourite, and takes different forms; typically, it consists of two concentric diamond shapes with lines extending from the corners, terminating in crosses and/or tridents, but the Stockholm MS shows a circular version. The Huld MS has one with radial spokes terminating in square tridents, very similar to the Helm of Awe.

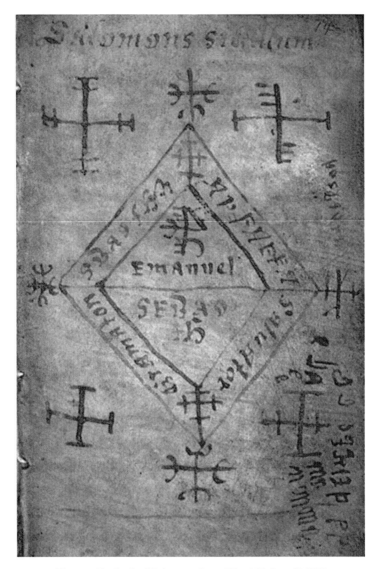

Figure 13: Seal of Solomon from Lbs 143 8vo (1670)

In no cases do they include the intersecting triangles of the 'Star of David', and it would seem that Icelandic magicians developed their own, idiosyncratic variations of this famous seal. There are also seals of Christ, the Holy Spirit, the Holy Trinity, David, Jareb (son of Solomon) and Joshua, and of the angels Anael, Gabriel, Michael, Raphael and Sachiel. All of these seals are explicitly or implicitly intended to be used as protective talismans.

In addition, there are appeals to God, Christ and the Holy Trinity in the prayers and incantations that are to be said; the Lord's Prayer and certain psalms feature in some. Six spells invoke King Olaf (Olaf II Haraldsson (995-1030), later known as Saint Olaf) for protection, the resolution of disputes and even for luck in gaming. One sleep-thorn spell (number 42 in Lbs 2413 8vo) overtly invokes 'the Devil'; this I have included in the category of purely Judeo-Christian references even though, by a syncretic process, the Christian Devil had become confused with Loki by this time.

Of particular interest are the spells – a small minority - that call upon the gods of the old Nordic pantheon. Quite often, they are invoked together with Christ, God, the Virgin Mary or the Holy Trinity without any apparent sense of irony, but in five cases only Heathen gods are mentioned. Among all the spells that are the subject of this study, the Nordic gods and other entities invoked are (in order of frequency) Óðinn, Þór, Baldur, Freyja, Friggja, Týr, Loki, Hænir, Fjölnir, Jöfrir, Þórir, Þumill, Örvandill, Hringþornir, Hliðskjálfargramur, Freyr, Njörður, Birgir, Gefun, Gusta, the Æsir in general, and the Elves. The spells that invoke Heathen gods have an unusually high ratio of malign intent, which perhaps says something about how the elder pantheon was regarded by the early modern period, but it should be noted that two spells of benign intent – one to discover the thief, the other to make a thief return stolen goods – fall into the 'Heathen only' category. Another point to mention is that the spells invoking Heathen gods all tend to do so with a degree of conviction that is often lacking in the purely Judeo-Christian category, especially those of the latter which only include 'dog Latin'.

As already stated, there is a sizeable overlap between the use of a magical stave or image and an appeal to a supernatural power[31], so the categories are by no means exclusive. Having dealt with these two main themes, we can now move on to the techniques that were most commonly used.

Talismans

Talismans and amulets are types of magical spells that are designed to be worn or carried by a person for a certain amount of time – often permanently – in order to achieve their effect. They may also be hung on domestic animals or affixed to houses. The terms are frequently regarded as interchangeable, but for present purposes I will use 'talisman' to describe a magical object that bears an

---

[31] For those who would like the exact statistics (as accurately as I can ascertain them), the figures break down as follows:
No appeal to supernatural power or use of sign/image:12
Appeal to supernatural power, no sign/image:50
Appeal to supernatural power and sign/image:75
Sign/image without appeal to supernatural power:224

inscription such as letters, runes or a magical sign or image, and 'amulet' to describe one that bears no such inscription, such as a stone, a hare's foot or some more complex object. Only one of the spells in these six books takes the form of an amulet, and that is the last one recorded in the Stockholm MS:

> "How one can get the helm of hiding
> If you want to make the helm of hiding for yourself, take a hen's egg and put blood into it from under the big toe of your left foot. Then put the egg under the bird and let it hatch. Then take the chick and burn it on oak wood, then put it into a linen bag and carry it on your head."

Talismans, on the other hand, are numerous and make up over a third of the magical operations encountered in the books. Sometimes they include only a line or two of written letters, and at other times an entire prayer, but most commonly they take the form of a magical stave or image drawn or carved onto some surface or other that is convenient to carry. They can be used to achieve a variety of effects. Apotropaic talismans tend to predominate, being intended to give long-term protection to the owner against danger of various kinds, from evil magic and spirits to attack by living enemies. Some, such as the 'Nine circles of aid' (níu hjálparhringar) in Lbs 143 8vo 'Galdrakver', offer very wide-ranging protection.

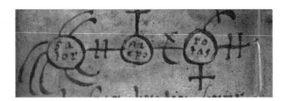

Figure 14: Nine Circles of Aid, Lbs 143 8vo

Other long-term objectives include luck, popularity, safe travel, success in trading, preventing theft, and winning in sports and games. On the other hand, there are talismans that are designed to achieve a specific, short-term purpose such as winning a lawsuit or otherwise defeating an enemy. Staves to inflict fear on an enemy are included in three of the books, and they are to be carried on one's person or held in the hand when expecting to meet the enemy. The staves for this purpose take a wide variety of shapes.

One set of talismanic staves may be of particular interest to the modern reader and scholar. It is listed in ÍB 383 4to, the 'Huld' MS, and the two staves are to be born on the left breast in order to focus the mind. They are given below; please feel free to try them out. I have written them onto a slip of paper and pinned them to the shirt over my left breast while writing this book, and I find they work, so I can enter them into my personal *galdrabók* with the comment that one sometimes sees in the old grimoires: *mun duga* – will work!

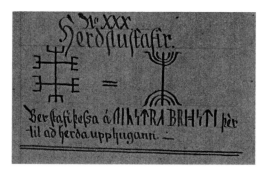

Figure 15: Item XXX from Huld MS

Once again, I have to emphasise that my attempts to categorise the aspects of Icelandic magic do not imply any clear-cut differences of approach. The creation of a talisman could involve many other factors, from the selection of the tool for scribing and the material for scribing on, to the part of the body where the talisman is to be worn or carried. Quite often, a prayer was to be said aloud and then carried as a talisman. There will always be 'grey' areas of overlap, but some discernment is necessary in order to identify the main trends.

The importance of incantation

Many of the magical operations are accompanied by the speaking of certain words; indeed, in some cases an incantation or prayer is the only apparent means by which the aim is accomplished. The specified incantations are sometimes vague ("… and say what you will") and often extremely terse ("say Morsa Orsa Dorsa"), but they can also extend to lengthy recitations with a metre, rhyme and alliteration that is lost in translation. Take, for example, this fragment from an incantation to banish a ghost[32]:

"Meinar þú morðinginn
mér nokkuð granda,
frá Guði ég sveia þér
ofan til fjanda.
Þar kvalirnar þér mest,
þúsund neta smiður,
í helvítið heitt of breitt,
halda þér niður."

(Do you, murderer,
intend to kill me?
From God I damn you
down to the Devil.
May the torture there,
you maker of a thousand nets,
in a hot and wide hell,
hold you down.)

Incantation is, of course, at the very heart of Nordic magic; the very word for magic in Icelandic, *galdur*, is derived from *að gala*, to chant, and in the Hattatal section of the Prose Edda, Snorri Sturluson devotes a section to *galdralag*, or 'incantation metre'. Dillmann argues effectively

---

[32] Lbs 2413 8vo, number 184 'Draugastefna'; translation by Magnús Rafnsson.

that magical incantations, as described in the sagas, were beautiful, harmonious and pleasing to the ear, even when of malign intent[33]. It may therefore be the case that other magical workings included some form of incantation, even where this is not explicitly stated, and that the sorcerer was expected to compose his own verses to accompany the carving of a stave. As already said, we are working here from aide-memoires rather than full books of instruction.

Incantation could constitute the main method of a working, but be accompanied by certain other actions, such as ritual washing and visualisation in the *Ægishjálmur* spells that are discussed in more detail in chapter 9. Many of the 'prayers' that are included in the grimoires may really be taken as incantations, for however much they appeal to a higher power, the tenor of their text is to compel a result by the power of incantation.

The methods of delivery

This brings us to the methods by which the magical intent is delivered to the object, beneficiary or victim that it is intended to influence. We have already looked at talismanic magic, where the aim is usually achieved by hanging a magically-charged object on the person himself or his property (livestock or house), and we have touched on the subject of incantation, whereby the effect might – in some cases – be brought about solely by saying well-crafted words. Talismanic magic almost always implies compliance

---

[33] Francois-Xavier Dillmann, "Les Magiciens dans l'Islande Ancienne", Uppsala 2006, p. 121.

on the part of the bearer of the talisman, and that is one reason that the majority of talismans are apotropaic, i.e. intended to protect from evil. Now we must examine the other methods by which a working might be put in place, especially in those cases where the target will be anything but compliant. The dimension of space is the major factor here, and five major categories can be identified:

a) Carving directly onto a tool, beast, person or other object;

b) Bringing the prepared spell into contact with the target;

c) Ingestion by the target;

d) Bringing the prepared spell into proximity with the target;

e) Working at a distance.

This is a very tricky subject to analyse, as the following example will illustrate. It is spell number 74 from Lbs 2413 8vo:

> "To let your enemy come at your will, make these staves in the left palm with blood from the same arm and make the sign of the cross in the same direction. The staves come here."

Figure 16: Item 74, Lbs 2413 8vo

The sorcerer therefore draws blood from his own left arm and uses it to draw the staves on his own left palm, then signs a cross in the direction, presumably, that he wants his enemy to come from. There is an element of direct 'carving' (on the sorcerer's palm) and of contact (with the sorcerer himself), but the power of the spell is exerted over a distance to make his enemy arrive at a time and place of his choosing.

For this reason, we will focus on the target of the spell, sometimes at the expense of other factors.

Direct carving

In some respects, this method bears many similarities to talismanic magic. 'Carving', as already mentioned, did not always mean the literal carving of a sign into a surface, but frequently it did – especially when a tool was to be charmed in order to work more effectively. Staves could be cut into whetstones to make them put a better edge on a cutting instrument, and faster. Other staves might be cut into the rowlocks or keel of a fishing boat, or onto the line sinker, in order to ensure a good catch. Different ones could also be secretly carved into the same places (the rowlocks or the keel) on a competitor's boat to prevent him from catching fish. Direct carving could also be used, in two instances, to magically hide an object from the sight of those seeking it. One of the staves for this purpose is called *augnaþurs* (eye-giant), which reveals something about the nature of its working – to unleash the chaotic and disruptive thursic force upon the eye to baffle and blind.

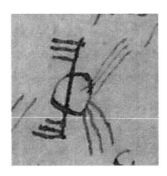

Figure 17: augnaþurs from Lbs 2413 8vo

It must be said that objects could also be charmed by other means, without carving, as revealed by one spell in AM 434 a 12mo 'Lækningakver', in which dice are charmed to fall in one's favour by a complex process involving place, time and invocation. (For details of this spell, see chapter 10.)

Direct carving onto oneself or livestock can in some cases be regarded as creating an 'instant talisman' that will be effective for a limited period and for a specific purpose. If, for example, the sorcerer wished to protect himself, he could trace a sign onto his own skin (most often the forehead or the palm of the hand) using a finger, sometimes with spittle. The spells that are designed to protect livestock by putting magical staves onto the animal itself do not specify exactly how they are to be carved, but some other spells intended to heal them or cure them of evil magic specify branding, writing with a pencil or clipping the sign into the fur using scissors. By inference, we may assume that these methods could also be used to protect livestock, though it may be that the 'finger and spittle' method was also sometimes used. Such 'instant talismans' were not necessarily apotropaic. They could also be used to soothe anger, win card games, and gain victory in lawsuits.

Magical staves and words could also be traced directly onto the target to heal, to harm or to seduce. An example can be found in spell number 41 of Lbs 2413 8vo:

> "To damage a horse with a man riding on it. Carve on the loin with the long finger of your left hand."

Figure 18: Item 41, Lbs 2413 8vo

It may be assumed that the intention here is to cause the horse to falter and stumble, thereby throwing the rider. To achieve this, the sorcerer had to get close enough to the horse at some point in order to trace the stave on the loin with his finger. This would have left no visible mark and the rider would have mounted and ridden, unsuspecting, to an apparent 'accident'.

Bringing a prepared spell into direct contact with the target

Like direct carving, this method called for an opportunity to come into very close contact with the target, and it was therefore a favourite for 'love' spells. A stave might, for instance, be traced on your own palm with spittle and then you would subsequently shake hands with the object of your desire, transferring the magical energy and making the girl fall in love with you. The same method of delivery could be used to influence an enemy, though it must be observed that the enemy could not have been implacably hostile if he were prepared to shake hands! Staves could also be carved on some other material such as wood, whalebone, paper or vellum, and then brought into direct contact with the target of the magic: a love spell calls for the stave to be drawn on sanctified paper and placed under the woman's hand; a spell to make someone lose his way is to be prepared and then attached to the victim; another, 'lock breaker', is to be inserted into the lock and then certain words spoken, at which the lock will burst asunder; and in the case of one of the notorious 'farting' spells, the staves are to be carved on a slip of wood and placed into the victim's trousers. These are only some examples. Because of the element of subterfuge and breach of trust, many of the spells employing this method are of malign intent.

Ingestion

There is a category, covering thirteen spells in all, which could also be considered as working by direct contact, but is sufficiently different to be worth mentioning. In these workings, the staves or words are carved in advance and then given to target as food or drink. In many cases, they are carved on cheese, bread or fish and then offered to the victim, but in two cases they are carved on another material (unspecified in one and 'killing oak' (*drápseik*) in another) and then somehow mixed into a drink. There are two cases where the intention is to heal, and cheese or parchment is consumed voluntarily. In the majority, however, the aim is to harm or compel. Spells employing ingestion as the method of delivery are used to heal, to gain a girl's love, to cause pregnancy, to impose silence, to make someone become a thief, to test virginity and to inflict vomiting. The idea of mixing magic into a drink is an ancient one in Nordic myth. There is the mead of poetry and wisdom, which Odin worked so hard to retrieve from the giant Suttung's hoard, and in Sigrdrifumál the Valkyrie says of the runes:

> "All were shaved off, those which were carved on,
> and scattered with the sacred mead
> and sent on wandering ways..."

Delivery by proximity

All the aforementioned workings involve direct contact with the target: either the material from which an inanimate object is made, or the tissue of a living being. The next category to consider is of spells which work by proximity, without direct contact. The degree of proximity is often so close as to almost count as direct contact, but the wording of the spell indicates that something, at least, lies between the sorcerer (or his creation) and the recipient. As examples of such close proximity we may take the numerous workings in which a carved stave is placed under the head of a sleeping person or on the bedclothes. We may justifiably assume that at least a pillow lies between the piece of wood and the sleeper's head, otherwise it would be felt or seen, and the victim would awake even if already sleeping. Placing a magic object under an enemy's head to charm him into an unnatural continuation of sleep, to make him reveal his secrets or to otherwise change his disposition appears to have been a favourite method. One might also sleep on a magical charm of one's own making to get the dreams – perhaps divinatory – that one wanted.

In other operations, there is absolutely no doubt that the spell took effect in the presence of the target, but with some intervening physical distance. An incantation could be spoken over a woman to ease childbirth. Magical staves could be carved on the bedpost of a prospective lover to make her fall in love with you, or make sure that nobody else took her virginity before you had the chance to do so. They could also be deposited somewhere along the route that the target was likely to take, taking effect when the target, or targets, stepped over them, or carved on the threshold of a house so that a thief would be trapped within and unable to leave. An enemy's sheep could be driven wild by carving a stave on beech wood and then waving it while standing upwind of the flock. Most of these operations, it seems, were to be done secretly (indeed many spells specify that the victim must be 'unknowing' (óvitandi)), but in a handful of cases they were apparently meant to be done overtly, as in the 'Terror Stave' (*óttastafur*) spell in the Huld MS:

> "Carve this stave on an oaken tablet and cast it before your enemy's feet in order to terrify him."

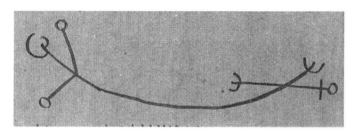

Figure 19: Óttastafur from Huld MS

The interesting thing about the proximity-based spells is that the energy generated for the magical intention is transferred without physical contact, frequently in the absence of the sorcerer, to an unknowing target. This demonstrates the belief that the staves of a working could radiate a 'magical field' that was attuned to a specific target or targets.

Delivery from a distance

Even more intriguing, from the aspect of magical transference of energy, are those spells that operate over a considerable distance to take effect on the target. Sometimes these work by incantation only, as in a spell to stem the flow of blood from Lbs 434 a 12mo 'Lækningakver', which begins:

> "You may send this blood-stanching **anywhere you want**, as soon as you know the name of the man or the appearance of the animal:

May your blood be stanched † in nomine patris et filii et spiritus amen[34]."

However, it is more common for an incantation to be combined with the carving of a stave, and occasionally the stave alone suffices. A good example of a stave in combination with an incantation is the vomiting spell recorded (number 186) in Lbs 2413 8vo. To give an idea of the alliterative quality of the incantation, part of it is quoted in Icelandic below:

> "Up skaltu spýja átu þinni, svo skal búkur þinn böls fullur vera. Nú skulu gaula garnir þínar en kettir illir þig klóri innan."

> (Up you will throw your food and so shall your body be full of misfortune. May your intestines cry and evil cats scratch your insides.)

---

[34] Lest it be thought that incantations of 'Christian' origin were used only with benign intent, it should be noted that Lbs 143 8vo and the Stockholm MS both include the 109th Psalm as means of cursing by way of retribution. It is worth quoting verses 8 to 13 in order to remind ourselves of its utter vindictiveness:
"Let his days be few;
And let another take his office.
Let his children be fatherless,
And his wife a widow.
Let his children be continually vagabonds, and beg:
Let them seek their bread also out of their desolate places.
Let the extortioner catch all that he hath;
And let the strangers spoil his labour.
Let there be none to extend mercy unto him:
Neither let there be any to favour his fatherless children.
Let his posterity be cut off;
And in the generation following let their name be blotted out."

Like three of the 'farting spells', which use runes together with incantations, this was clearly intended to operate at a distance from the victim, as was also the summoning spell quoted earlier in this chapter. Such an ability, to send a magical working across a considerable distance to an unseen target, implies an extraordinary measure of power and confidence on the part of the sorcerer.

The few instances of sympathetic magic [35] to be discovered in these books make up a final, small category that might be considered as being delivered at a distance. Unlike European witchcraft, with its creation of poppets and emphasis on arcane correspondences, sympathetic magic does not appear to have featured greatly in Icelandic magic. Two spells call for staves to be carved and placed in the hoof-print of someone's horse in order to either harm his livestock or kill him by falling from his horse; two other spells are for weather control, one to call up favourable winds, the other to call up a northern blizzard. For a better

---

[35] In 'The Golden Bough', Sir James Frazer divides sympathetic magic into two categories, homeopathic (or imitative) magic, and contagious magic: "Perhaps the most familiar application of the principle that like produces like is the attempt which has been made by many peoples in many ages to injure or destroy an enemy by injuring or destroying an image of him, in the belief that, just as the image suffers, so does the man, and that when it perishes he must die... The other great branch of sympathetic magic, which I have called Contagious Magic, proceeds upon the notion that things which have once been conjoined must remain ever afterwards, even when quite dissevered from each other, in such a sympathetic relation that whatever is done to the one must similarly affect the other."

explanation of how sympathetic magic might work, let us take one of the first two, number 30 in the Stockholm MS:

"To kill another's livestock
One should write these staves on a leaf and cast it into his horse's hoof-print, then some of his livestock will die, if he offends you undeservedly, and hide the stave in the horse's hoof-print."

Figure 20: Item number 30, Stockholm MS

Though the clauses are a little garbled, this may be interpreted as follows: if someone has offended you undeservedly and you want revenge, write these staves on a leaf [or sheet of paper] and hide it in the place where his horse has trodden; then some of his livestock will die.

This is interesting, because the main target is the enemy's livestock, but there is no mention of whether this livestock is close by (unless it refers to the horse itself, but then one would expect the wording to be more specific). Nor does it imply that the horse and rider have to pass over the hidden staves; there is only association by means of a hoof-print that has already been made. If we assume that the livestock are sheep – which would be common in Iceland – the spell appears to work by the following associative path:

Sorcerer → staves → hoof-print → horse → rider → rider's sheep.

Not all of the workings contained in these six grimoires can be conveniently classified according to the distance over which they operate. Sometimes the nature of the working precludes this because the dimension of space is less relevant, and at other times the text of the instruction is so vague that it is impossible to make any assumptions.

Divination

There are twenty-four, possibly twenty-five, magical operations which relate to divination. The majority of these are for finding out who has stolen something, but some are for more general purposes. The main methods employed are oneiromancy (divination by dreaming) and scrying, but bibliomancy and the floating of lots are also used, and there are undoubtedly elements of necromancy in some of the spells. Where oneiromancy is employed, the technique almost invariably involves carving staves onto an object and then sleeping on it; a dream then tells the enquirer what he wishes to know. The stave-forms vary greatly, as do the specified carving instrument and the carved surface (we will go into greater detail concerning the tools of magic in a subsequent chapter).

The next most common method is scrying. Here, too, magical staves are usually employed, and they are carved on the inside of a vessel, which is then filled with water. When the diviner looks into the water-filled vessel, he is supposed to see the face of the thief. A vessel filled with water could also be used to float slips of paper with the names of the main suspects written on them; the name that sank first was assumed to give away the identity of the thief.

The spells listed as number 13 and 14 in the second part of 'Tvær Galdraskræður' (Lbs 764 8vo) appear to form two parts of the same spell, which works by bibliomancy (divination from writing in a book). Number 14 reads:

> "Everything you would most like to know
> Then you can sing a psalm from the Psalter and choose it and random. The letter on the page you open and is the first in the third line on the right hand should show your life how it will be."

Spell 13, on the previous page, gives a list of 24 letters from A to Æ, as per the Icelandic alphabet (but omitting Ð, J, V, Ö, and Þ), together with associated predictions such as 'longevity', 'good life' and 'joy'. Some of the predictions are duplicated. The divination is also accompanied by a fairly complex stave, but how this comes into the divination exercise is unclear.

One spell in the Stockholm MS seems to employ necromancy (divination by consulting the dead), though the wording does not make clear how the information is to be imparted:

> "To find a thief

Carve this on shrub-oak and lay it under the turf on top of a grave, and let it lie there."

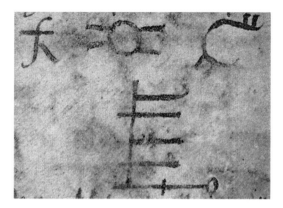

Figure 21: Item 36, Stockholm MS

There is perhaps also an element of necromancy in the oneiromantic spell number 44 in Lbs 764 8vo, in that the staves are to be carved on a dead man's skull.

Note that these are the only methods of divination mentioned in the six grimoires. There is absolutely no mention of divination by other means such as runes, dice, Tarot cards or playing cards.

Ritual washing

Washing rituals are mentioned in two of the books, once in AM 434 a 12mo 'Lækningakver' and three times in the Stockholm MS. In general terms, the purpose of the ritual was to wash away the scorn and wrath of powerful men, to avert lawsuits and bring general protection and good luck. Three of them mention the Ægishjálmur (helm, or cloak, of awe) being borne 'between the brows'. Presumably, this stave was visualised. An interesting factor is that the wording of spell number 26 in the Stockholm MS is virtually identical to the one in 'Lækningakver', even though latter predates this section of the Stockholm MS by about a hundred years. Perhaps the person who wrote the second section of the later grimoire had access to the earlier one at some point, or it may be that this washing ritual was widely known.

Though the list is not exhaustive, these make up the main techniques of Icelandic magic as evidenced by six separate grimoires.

Conclusions

It is beyond doubt that the magic of early modern Iceland was mainly characterised by the use of signs and images, and that an extraordinary amount of faith was invested in their efficacy. As the reader will have discerned from the examples shown in the illustrations, these signs and images are very varied in form but are 'typically Icelandic' in that they are rarely encountered elsewhere in the world. Quite often, the carving of the stave alone is sufficient to accomplish the magical intention, though they were more frequently accompanied by other actions such as incantation, visualisation and appeals to a supernatural power. Sometimes incantation alone (usually with an appeal to supernatural entities) was used, but such instances are vastly outnumbered by the spells in which staves *were* used. Modern practitioners of Rune magic may be surprised – and perhaps a little disappointed – to find that the Futhark Runes played hardly any role in the magic of this period. Except in a very few spells, they are used only to encrypt the text of the instructions. As might be expected by around 1600 CE, six centuries after the conversion of Iceland to Christianity, most appeals to a supernatural power are of a Judeo-Christian nature, though in some cases they invoke the Devil, Satan, Beelzebub and/or the gods of the old Nordic pantheon, such as Odin and Thor. The true *galdur* tradition of magic in the saga era persisted in the incantations, though the incantations were often conceived (or perhaps disguised) as prayers. On occasions, the specified incantation is well crafted and alliterative, but in many cases it consists of no more than a few words of dog Latin, probably filched and corrupted from Catholic liturgy. However, it may be that incantation made up a more important element than the text of the grimoires would indicate, and that a simple injunction to 'say what you will' was taken by the user to mean that he should craft some poetic lines of his own.

The magical energy invested in the carving of a stave could be transmitted by a variety of means, from direct carving onto an object, person or animal to transmission over a considerable distance. In many cases, the intention was transferred to a talisman that was worn or held to achieve its effect, but in many others the willed intention was reinforced by certain actions, embodied in a stave, and then transferred to the target over a greater or lesser distance. Divination also forms a major category among the operations, and this is dominated by oneiromancy and scrying. Even these operations most often employed some kind of stave.

It can therefore truly be said that Icelandic magic in this period primarily involved the use of staves and images of varied types and forms. We will return to these types and forms, and the possibility of interpreting them, in a later chapter.

CHAPTER 5

THE TOOLS OF ICELANDIC MAGIC

If the six grimoires available for this study are anything to go by, the tools used for magic in early modern Iceland were usually simple in the extreme. Very rarely was anything required that might require elaborate preparation – there is no mention of special clothing, of casting of circles, or of wands, swords or pentacles. In most cases, in fact, nothing is required that could not readily be found among the everyday equipment and belongings of the average farmer. As has already been established in the previous chapter, Icelandic magic relied heavily on the carving of staves, and most of the tools relate to this practice. On the other hand, it will be seen that some instances can be discovered where elaborate preparation was necessary, and these are rather interesting when social and economic circumstances are borne in mind.

The carving instrument

Because we are now really getting down to the practicalities, I wish to emphasise yet again that interpretation of language is a crucial issue[36]. The verb most commonly used to describe the scribing of the staves is *að rista*, to carve, even when the context shows that literal carving cannot be intended. Other verbs used are *að skrifa*, to write, and *að gjöra / að gera*, to make. 'Carve' is therefore intended here to denote all methods of tracing a stave, even when a pen or a finger was used. In most cases where a stave or image was to be made, the carving instrument is not specified; fewer than 25% of such spells make any clear stipulation.

Fingers

Quite often, one of the sorcerer's fingers would suffice, either dry, or wetted with blood or saliva (we will return to the matter of body fluids later). From analysis of these spells, a clear pattern emerges. A finger was often used when the surface to be 'carved' was the magician's own skin, or in circumstances where instant magic was required – and the urgency therefore took precedence over the availability of tools – or where secrecy was a necessity, so no visible mark was to be left. Three spells can be cited by way of illustration. The first is from Lbs 143 8vo 'Galdrakver':

> "This symbol shall be drawn on the forehead using the index finger and one's mouth water, while fasting, if one is expecting to confront an enemy."

---

[36] I hope to make a separate study of the language of Icelandic magic at some point in the future.

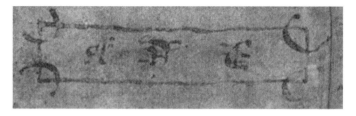

Figure 22: Item 20 from Lbs 143 8vo 'Galdrakver'

The intention here is to protect the magician himself against his enemy. The stave was traced with saliva on his own forehead using the index finger, though there is no indication whether the right or left hand was to be used. The criterion 'while fasting' would most likely indicate that it was to be performed at the start of the day, before breakfast, and from this we may infer that the magician had at least some time to prepare in advance. Two factors are therefore important in the choice of a finger for carving: a) the surface is the magician's own skin, and b) it is possible that he would not want a visible mark to show when meeting his enemy.

The second is from Lbs 2413 8vo:

> "If you want to win at gaming, you should carve this stave in your palm using your finger and mouth water."

Figure 23: Item 136, Lbs 2413 8vo

Here we may imagine the magician unexpectedly finding himself in a game of cards or dice; he has had no opportunity to prepare a more elaborate talisman, so in order to win, he wets his finger with saliva and traces the stave on his palm.

The third is also from Lbs 2413 8vo and is a love charm:

> "To get a girl. Carve in her palm with your finger and say: Morsa Orsa Dorsa."

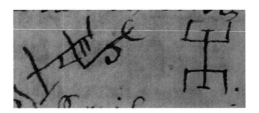

Figure 24: Item 13, Lbs 2413 8vo

The magician with amorous intent therefore has to be close enough to the girl – one may picture him sitting next to her and pretending to idly tickle her palm – in order to secretly trace the staves before uttering the macaronic incantation "Morsa Orsa Dorsa", at which she will fall ineluctably in love with him. Of course, one may argue that the mission was already halfway accomplished if the girl was comfortable enough in his presence to allow him to sit tickling her palm!

Even when it is not directly stated that a finger should be used to trace the stave, this sometimes appears to be the obvious solution; for example "That an enemy fear you. Make this stave with your saliva in your left palm."

In some cases, a specific finger is stipulated. Two spells stipulate the index finger, but without saying on which hand; both of these spells are associated with protection against enemies or to soothe the anger of enemies (one is a 'Helm of Awe' working). Two more specify the leech (ring) finger of the left hand, one of them being to avert magic and the other to get friendship. Although the ring finger of the left hand was called the 'leech', or healing, finger (*græðifingur*), it is not used for healing magic anywhere in these six books. It is possible, however, that further exploration among other grimoires will turn up evidence that it was used for this purpose. One spell stipulates use of the long finger of the left hand, and this spell is to damage a horse while a man is riding it[37].

Knives, awls and scissors

Where literal carving is required, a knife is commonly specified. This is usually one's *mathníf* (literally 'food-knife') – the knife that one customarily uses when eating. It may have also been used for other things, and most people probably carried a general-purpose knife with them at all times. By virtue of daily use, this would have a strong psychic link with the owner. Where the carved staves were to be stained with blood, logic dictates that it could also be used to draw the blood, though this is never actually stipulated; most of the spells where use of the eating-knife is specified do not call for staining with blood. A higher than normal proportion of spells involving use of one's eating-

---

[37] See Chapter 4 under 'Direct carving'.

knife are of malign or neutral intent, i.e. designed to harm, to affect a person's free will or to gain an advantage over others.

On occasions, the spell instructions call for something more specialised: a thief-finding spell in the Stockholm MS calls for the stave to be carved on the bottom of the scrying-bowl with a knife with a wooden handle; two of the workings in Lbs 2413 8vo require that the runes or stave should be carved with an unused knife; and a talisman (probably apotropaic) described in the same book is to be carved on oak using a copper knife. The last three, especially, are among the few spells to be found that require something out of the ordinary in the way of physical equipment. Most people in early modern Iceland were very poor by today's standards, and they could ill afford to have unused tools lying around. Tools were used again and again until utterly worn out, and only then replaced. Unless a knife happened to have been purchased for normal purposes and not yet used, a new one would have to be specially procured, perhaps made by a local blacksmith, for the express purpose of performing the spell. It would therefore have been a luxury, diverting funds from the small amount of available income. A copper knife would have been even more unusual; copper does not hold an edge well, and a copper knife would have been almost useless for anything other than magical purposes. These cases tell us that, on rare occasions, Icelandic magical practice was similar to that of other traditions in specifying the use of 'virgin' implements that are untainted by everyday use. One spell in the Stockholm MS goes even further in requiring a special hammer, but because this operation is worth dwelling on in detail, we will come back to it in chapter 10. Instead of a knife, some spells stipulate the use of a needle or an awl. Like eating-knives, awls would have been fairly commonplace items in any toolbox, used for marking wood or making holes in leather. As with knives, however, the spells occasionally specify an awl made of some unusual material, and we will deal with these in a later section.

Finally, there are two spells, one in Lbs 2413 8vo and one in Lbs 764 8vo, which call for clipping with scissors. In both of them, a stave is to be made on a living animal in order to cure it; it seems safe to assume that the stave is to be clipped into the hair or wool of the animal in question.

Pens, pencils and chalk

More 'modern' instruments of writing were not entirely eschewed, and some of the spells say that one should use a pen, a pencil or, in one case, chalk. It should remembered that our word pen and the Icelandic *penni* are both derived from the Latin *penna*, meaning the wing-feather of a bird, and such hand-cut quills were the only type of pen available until metal dip-pens emerged in the early 19th Century. Given that many birds have esoteric associations (for example, the heron is associated with Frigg and the hawk with Freya), it may be that there is more to the use of quill pens than meets the eye. One talismanic spell for luck in gaming specifies that the stave should be written with a raven's feather, which may possibly indicate a connection with Odin. Quills from a number of bird species would have been readily available to Icelanders, as they are discarded naturally and can also be gained from hunted birds or carrion.

In two cases, blood is prescribed for writing with, but by the seventeenth century, local recipes for ink had been developed, and one of these has been described as follows:

> "Bearberry was used for making ink. It was boiled in an iron pot with sticks of unbudded willow, undoubtedly to extract some kind of tannin or resin. A black dye made from humus was added to darken the ink. This was otherwise used for dying clothes and derived its black colour from the presence of iron sulphate. Its surface properties were ideal when a drop placed on the fingernail held its form; this meant it would not spread on the vellum but penetrate well into it.[38]"

The pencil, in its modern form, has been around for a surprisingly long time, having been invented in Italy around 1560 CE. The Icelandic word for pencil, *blýantur*, perpetuates the erroneous connection of graphite with lead, as does our commonly used term 'lead pencil'. As any artist knows, graphite comes in many degrees of hardness. The medium-hard 'HB' pencil is today favoured for ordinary writing on paper, but softer variations are more useful for writing on other surfaces, such as metal or skins. In my opinion, these softer grades would have been the type preferred by the average Icelandic farmer or fisherman. In any case, pencils would have been relatively luxurious items – certainly

---

[38] Soffía Guðný Guðmundsdóttir and Laufey Guðnadóttir, "Book production in the Middle Ages" in "The Manuscripts of Iceland", Reykjavík 2004.

compared to quill pens – as they could not be manufactured locally and had to be imported. In the few spells where they are mentioned, they are used for writing on wood, on sanctified paper, or on the hide of a living animal.

Finally, chalk is mentioned in one spell in the Stockholm MS, which is of considerable age. The stave is to be chalked on the crossbeam of one's house in the course of a thief-finding operation. Although the kind of chalk sticks which we take for granted these days were not available until the 19th Century, gypsum (calcium sulphate) does occur naturally in Iceland, being deposited by thermal springs.

Materials used for carving

Except where otherwise stipulated (as in the case of the copper knife mentioned above), knives would usually have been made of steel. Even so, this seems not to have been taken for granted, and a number of the spells very specifically state that one should carve with steel. It is therefore tempting to look for some kind of arcane correspondence, in the same way that iron is associated with Mars in the Western Tradition. However, it is difficult to draw any hard conclusion regarding its use, as the purposes of the spells vary widely. Iron is widely credited with apotropaic powers in folklore, and it is possible that carving with steel was intended to ward off any interference with the spell's purpose from supernatural beings (e.g. elves) or another sorcerer.

Other materials are also mentioned in the spells. In addition to the one calling for the use of a copper knife, there are two others stating that one should carve with copper or brass. In these three cases, we may tentatively discern some kind of correspondence: two of them are for creating apotropaic talismans, and the third is for healing colic. They can therefore all be categorised as 'of benign intent'. Beyond that, however, nothing certain can be said on the basis of but three examples, and staves with the same or similar intentions were also carved with other materials.

Awls or other implements of silver and lead feature in some spells and, once again, for varying intentions. For example, a silver awl could be used to carve on the lintel of a house for protection against evil spirits, while the edge of a silver coin (plus one's saliva) was used to carve a talisman on headgear in order to bring popularity; lead was used in one spell to carve an apotropaic talisman, in another to carve a stave on the bottom of a bowl in preparation for scrying the identity of a thief.

On one occasion, it is specified that one should carve with wood (as an alternative to lead in the aforesaid thief-scrying exercise), and an awl made of juniper is suggested as an alternative to one of silver for the lintel-carving against evil spirits. Juniper is mentioned in the Icelandic folk tales of Jón Árnason – mainly in connection with its antipathy to rowan – but there is no mention of it being used as protection against evil spirits.

Human bones could also be used for carving, and they were presumably whittled to a point for this purpose. Three spells specify human bones as the carving instrument, or suggest them as one of the options, and all three are of malign (or a fairly suspect 'neutral') intent. A human finger bone could be used as an alternative to an unused knife in the previously mentioned fart-rune spell; in fact, this option is mentioned first and may have been the preferred one. Another spell, for trading, also prescribes that the stave should be carved with a human finger bone; the stave was to be traced in your own blood on the skin of a cow's first calf, and then the sign was to be held as you made the sign of the cross 'backwards' over the person you were trading with while uttering an incantation (presumably at a distance and without the knowledge of the trading partner). A third, for victory in wrestling (*glíma*), instructs: "*Carve these staves on your shoe with human bone or a toe-bone from the foot that you wrestle with, and say 'I send the Devil himself into the breast and bone of the one who wrestles with me, in your names, Thor and Odin', and turn your face to the north-west.*" The idea of carving with a toe-bone from one's favoured foot is even more intriguing than the use of a bone from a dead man, as this would be potentially crippling! However, there is nothing in the text to suggest that it first had to be detached from the foot; perhaps it was sufficient to prick a toe to draw blood and then trace the staves with the toe.

Basalt, lignite and horn are also mentioned among the materials used for carving, each on one occasion only. Yet again, no direct connection can be made between the material and the purpose, as the same purpose could be served just as well with other materials. However, a small ray of hope shines through for those looking for homeopathic magic: in Lbs 2413 8vo there is a talismanic stave against seasickness.

"Carve this stave on the skin of a heifer with your blood. Carve with the foremost spine of a dogfish to cure seasickness, and carry on your person."

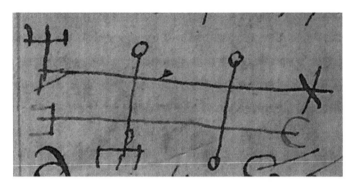

Figure 25: Item 97, Lbs 2413 8vo

The spiny dogfish (*Squalus Acanthias*) is native to Icelandic coastal waters (and elsewhere), and it may be that the intention was to cure seasickness by association with a creature that has its home in the sea. In October 2008, a friend of mine, Hermann, invited me to join him on his trawler in the waters off northern Iceland. Despite the choppy sea, which rolled the boat in a corkscrew motion, I was not seasick. He expressed his admiration, saying "For the first two years when I went to sea, I was seasick every time." I asked him why he had not given up and pursued another career, to which he replied "There was nothing else. It was fishing or nothing." It is a pity that he had not known of this talisman – it might have saved him a lot of misery!

The carved surfaces

The surfaces on which magical staves, images and runes were carved display even greater variety than the instruments used for carving them.

Clear choices

Where the direct carving method was employed (see Chapter 4), the surface was an obvious choice – one's own skin, the skin of another human, the hide or fur of an animal, a tool that was to be charmed or an object that was to be hidden from view. Where tools, such as fishing boats and whetstones, were to be charmed, some sharp instrument was almost invariably used to carve into the surface. Many of the workings for divination also fall into this category, as the purpose was to magically transform an ordinary bowl into one that could be used for scrying. (It should be mentioned at this point that some of these spells specify that the bowl should be new and unused.) For carving on the skin of a living person (the sorcerer's own or that of his target), a finger was generally used. To produce an 'instant talisman' the stave was often traced onto one's own forehead or the palm of a hand. In one case, a 'bargain sealer', two staves are used, one to be traced on one palm and the other onto the other palm. Staves could also be traced on one's own palm as a method of delivery. Most often, it is not specified whether the stave is to be made on the right or left palm, but when the charmed palm was to be offered in a handshake (in seduction spells, for example), it may be assumed that this was the palm of the right hand. A spell in the Stockholm MS would tend to confirm this:

"Likewise, while fasting, make the latter (helm of awe) with your spittle in your palm when you greet the girl whom you want to have. It should be the right hand."

Figure 26: Item 8 from Stockholm MS

The palm of the left hand is stipulated in two cases, one to summon an enemy, the other to inflict fear. However, the database is too small to say with any certainty that the 'sinister' hand was associated with spells of malign intent.

When some part of a living animal formed the surface to be carved, the exact position also varied. Staves could be carved on the sides or loin, the forehead, over the heart, or on a hoof. The specifications and the use of language indicate that this was usually done without harm or pain to the animal, by tracing with a finger or pencil, clipping into the hair or wool, or singeing of the wool, but in a couple of cases it seems that branding was used. The main criterion would appear to be the need for secrecy or otherwise; when a visible mark was to be left, it was generally to heal or protect an animal or make it compliant (indicating ownership), but if harm was intended, the stave was made with a finger or carved on the beast's hoof.

Direct carving aside, there are many other instances where the surface to be carved presents a fairly obvious choice. In spells to protect property against theft or to stop the thief getting away, staves could be carved at the doorway of one's home: on the lintel, the doorpost or the threshold step. Similarly, staves intended to seduce a girl or woman might be carved on her bedpost so that the magic would work on her as she slept, or on food such as bread or cheese, which she would then eat and unwittingly fall victim to the sorcerer. A horse might be harmed by carving staves on its saddle or saddle-cloth, so that the intention would work through by contact or direct proximity, or a man might be induced to become a thief by carving a stave on the bottom of his customary eating-plate, so that he absorbed the magic with each mouthful that he took.

In all the above cases, the choice of surface is self-explanatory, but there are many others where one must dig deeper to find an explanation. In the following section, we will look at some of the materials used when direct carving, contact or proximity was not necessarily required, and attempt to draw some conclusions. This is an interesting exercise, but very often the results are downright mystifying.

Wood

Wood was still the preferred surface on which to carve magical staves, and here we may assume that they were literally carved, rather than traced or written. A number of different tree species are stipulated in the grimoires – oak, beech, ash, pine, red spruce, Norway spruce, alder, birch and rowan. Of these, only birch and rowan are native to Iceland, with birch predominating by far. Despite that, rowan is mentioned only twice as the surface to be carved, and birch only once. The wood most often stipulated (in about 70% of cases) is oak, and this would have to have been imported, taken from salvaged ship hulks, or collected in the form of driftwood. The same applies to beech, alder and the coniferous trees cited above. There are a number of possible explanations for this. When I discussed the matter with Magnús Rafnsson, he put forward the opinion that 'oak' or 'beech' might be taken to mean "any substantial tree", including birch trees that had prospered and reached their full height. Another possibility is that these woods were valued precisely for their scarcity: that greater magical power was attached to a material that was difficult to procure. A third explanation is that the concept and folklore of these large, deciduous trees lived on in the language and traditions of Iceland, even though most Icelanders would never have seen a living specimen. A large body of folklore is attached to the oak in the Germanic and Celtic lands where it grows. For example, it is often associated with courage and stalwartness, as exemplified in the song 'Heart of Oak' and in the military awards and decorations of Germany, Great Britain and the U.S.A.

There are indications, too, that the oak was sacred to Donar (Thor) among the Germanic tribes, and the memory of this may have lived on among the descendants of the Norwegian settlers of Iceland. Oak is specified for many different intentions, and could be used to protect, to heal, to harm, or for divination. Some spells are even more specific in stipulating the use of *manndrápseik* ('killing oak' or 'manslaughter oak'). The precise nature of this is unknown, and one can only speculate as to what was meant by this. It is possible that it refers to wood salvaged from a fatal shipwreck. Despite its sinister name, however, it seems that such 'killing oak' could be used equally well for spells of a benign intent as for those with malign or neutral intent. Of four spells advocating the use of beech wood, on the other hand, two are of malign intent (one to harm livestock, the other to put the victim into a charmed sleep) and the other two are neutral, both being for advantage in trading.

When it comes to rowan, we are on firmer ground in Icelandic folklore. It is one of the few trees mentioned by name in the Prose Edda; Thor, on one of his journeys, grasps a rowan tree to haul himself out of a swollen river, and from this story, the rowan bears the by-name 'Thor's help' even today. The tree has associations of holiness and innocence in the folk tales, as well as protection against evil. Some Icelanders still plant rowans outside their homes for the latter purpose, and the two workings in the grimoires in which rowan is carved on are both for the creation of talismans against evil spirits.

Paper and parchment

As already mentioned in chapter 1, the advent of Christianity from the year 1000 onward brought a new emphasis on the written word, both for disseminating the new religion and for recording the laws of the country. With it came also the fashion for using the more convenient medium of parchment – carefully prepared pages made from calfskin – for writing on. At first, these were imported, but it was not long before Icelanders learned the craft and developed their own adaptations to suit the climate. Paper also made its appearance at a later date. These materials were also convenient for recording magical spells; indeed, were this not the case then we would not have these grimoires available to us today. A significant number of the operations described in the spell books specify that one should write staves on parchment or paper. Many of them stipulate that sanctified paper should be used, or the skin of a heifer or 'from a heifer's first calf'. As with the use of oak, it may be taken that a material which was more difficult to procure was held to have greater magical power. Sanctified paper would most likely have to be stolen from Church premises, and would be conceived as having intrinsic magical power because of its source. Similarly, the skin of a heifer or its first calf would have a certain rarity value in a pastoral economy where the ownership of cattle was something of a luxury compared to sheep. One spell instructs that the skin of a water rail (*rallus aquaticus*) should be used. This bird lives and breeds on marshy sites between land and water, and may have been prized for its liminal habitat.

In a few spells, the colour of the skin appears to have been important. The fart-rune spell from the Stockholm MS says that the runes should be written in one's own blood on white calfskin, while a 'dream stave' – to dream about one's chosen subject – in ÍB 383 4to 'Huld' states that the stave should be carved "on silver or white skin". Another, in Lbs 2413 8vo, is a protective talisman to be worn "when confronting evil spirits and darkness", and the staves are to be carved on "horse hide of a single colour". This is ambiguous, as it does not tell us whether the entire hide should be of a single colour, or only the piece that is used. Given the differences between the intentions of these three spells, no firm conclusion can be drawn regarding the significance of the colour, white, unmixed or otherwise. It is possible that the stipulation of silver or white skin in the Huld MS spell had some kind of lunar significance, but we can only speculate.

Metals

A restricted range of metals is also named among the surfaces to be carved. Understandably, these are all of the softer sort – brass, lead, silver and tin – otherwise it would be difficult to carve on them. Yet again, no firm correspondence can be established between the metal used and the end to which it is employed: it would appear that the same purpose could often be achieved by carving on a different metal, or on a different material entirely. The only inference that one can derive is that unused offcuts of metal would have been a rare commodity is a pre-industrial society. Today, a town dweller can beg a snippet of brass from a nearby factory or trophy manufacturer, or an old piece of roof flashing from a roofer, but such materials were rarely used in tool making or house construction in seventeenth-century Iceland. Precious metals such as silver would have been as costly (or more so) and difficult to procure as they are today. To use metals in the course of a magical working would therefore have required effort and a foregoing of income or personal treasure, making it a genuine sacrifice and adding to the power of the working. Little wonder, then, that spell number 172 in Lbs 2413 8vo is described as follows:

"The following seal, when carried, is powerful against all sorcery and all sendings by night and day. Scratch on scrap silver or lead, melted together, which is in clothing, chests, and everything marked in lead. Carve with brass or copper.[39]"

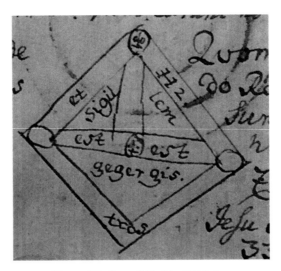

Figure 27: Item 172, Lbs 2413 8vo

One may imagine the sorcerer plundering his clothing of silver or pewter buttons, his furniture fittings, and anything else he can find in order to make an apotropaic talisman against other sorcerers. The sense of sacrifice has ever been an important component in the accomplishment of any aim, magical or otherwise.

---

[39] Translation Magnús Rafnsson, but with my emendations.

Bones, human and animal

Some workings require carving on bone. These are rather interesting and worth discussing in detail. Firstly, there is a spell in Lbs 2413 8vo to compel a sleeping man to tell you what you want to know:

> "Carve these staves on the hip of a mare with steel, and lay under his head to tell you what you want."

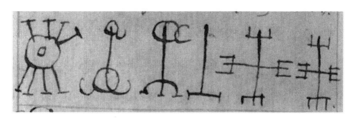

Figure 28: Item 44, Lbs 2413 8vo

Secondly, a spell apparently for divination by dreaming, from Lbs 764 8vo:

> "Carve these staves on the skull bone of a dead man and sleep on it; you will dream what you wish."

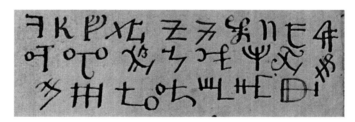

Figure 29: Item 44, Lbs 764 8vo

Thirdly, another spell from Lbs 2413 8vo, this time for skill in wrestling:

"If you want to win, then carve this stave on a human shoulder blade with steel, and keep it in the shoe of the leg you use for wrestling."

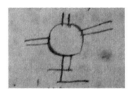

Figure 30: Item 70, Lbs 2413 8vo

Finally, a spell for thief-finding from the Stockholm MS:

"Carve this on a human (leg) bone and someone will come to you and spit out [i.e. speak forth] who took from you."

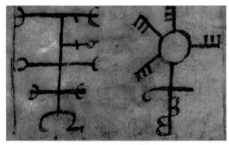

Figure 31: Staves from item 35, Stockholm MS

In the first spell, there is an association with the night-mare, a terrifying being common to many cultures, who invades the dreams of the sleeper and oppresses him or her. It would appear that the sorcerer harnesses the power of the mare, through the hip-bone of a dead, physical mare, to compel a sleeping man to render his secrets. I have come across charms against visitations from the night-mare before, but until now I have never seen the power of the mare used and directed in this manner.

The second relies on possession of a human skull, and carving staves upon it, in order to get divinatory dreams. Unlike some other oneiromantic spells, there is definitely a necromantic aspect to this operation; the use of a human skull clearly implies that the desired information was to emanate from the realm of the dead.

The third spell, for skill in wrestling, can be interpreted in two ways. It is possible that something has been omitted here, and that the piece of shoulder blade had to come from some famous wrestler now dead, so that his skills were sympathetically transmitted to the user. Alternatively, it may represent an attempt to combine the power of the shoulders with that of the foot; also, in wrestling it is necessary to keep one's centre of gravity low so as not to be easily overthrown, and this could also be the thought behind the spell – to bring the shoulder down to the level of the foot.

The last spell involves carving staves on a human bone in order to find out who the thief is. Someone comes to the sorcerer and discloses the identity of the thief. Although the instructions do not explicitly state it, this could be interpreted as raising the shade of a dead person to impart knowledge held only by the dead.

Sea creatures

The list of surfaces would not be complete without mentioning baleen (the keratinous filter material found in the mouths of certain whales). Two spells in Lbs 2413 8vo mention it: one is a 'sleep-thorn' type of spell to induce a charmed sleep; the other appears to be a necromantic working to discover a thief's identity and make him return the stolen goods. Whalebone is also used as a carved surface in a thief-finding spell in the Stockholm MS. Baleen and whalebone would not have been uncommon materials in Iceland. The country had its own whaling industry, and the bodies of stranded whales were fully exploited whenever they washed ashore.

One spell employs the 'shield' of a lumpfish (*rauðmagaskjöld*), presumably the bony carapace covering the gills, for the creation of a talisman for victory in lawsuits. Another involves using the head of a ling to bring up a northern gale:

> "To call up a northern blizzard. Carve this stave on the head of a ling and walk northwards, and wave it in the air."

Figure 32: Item 126, Lbs 2413 8vo

This would undoubtedly refer to the blue ling (*molva dypterygia*), which is native to Icelandic waters. The concept was most likely to insult and goad the weather-wights of the north by waving the head of such an ugly fish at them, thereby inviting retribution in the form of bad weather.

Use of body fluids and excretions

The use of body fluids, such as blood, saliva or semen, is a powerful element in many magical traditions. They can be used as a medium by which to send the magical intention, or to propitiate gods or other wights whose assistance is needed for the working, or to forge a sympathetic bond with the target of the magic. It therefore comes as something of a surprise that they are mentioned in fewer than one seventh of all the spells in these six books of magic. Even when we trim down the total to those that actually employ a stave, an image or runes (numbering about 300 individual spells), further activation with body fluids is mentioned in only 47 cases. Bearing in mind that the instructions in the grimoires are usually cursory, it is of course possible that this stage in the process was taken for granted and therefore omitted. Taken at face value, however, the evidence tends to go against the idea that staining the runes or staves was considered an essential part of the process.

Where visible staining was required, blood is the only medium that was used. There is no mention of special dyes being employed other than run-of-the-mill ink: no mention, for example, of red ochre or madder. (However, see the section on herbs and vegetable preparations below with regard to 'grape' juice and bilberries.) The blood that was used was usually the sorcerer's own, and in some cases it was to be drawn from a specific place on the body, the sites mentioned being the left arm, the left hand, the right side of the chest, the middle of the chest, the thigh, under the big toe, and under the tongue. These specific blood-letting sites are mentioned in only eight spells of widely varying intentions. With such a small source base (and considering that the same aims could apparently be accomplished without blood), it is impossible to draw conclusions as to their significance. The left side of the body – often considered nearer the heart and therefore more powerful – is cited in only four of the eight examples; if people then were, as now, predominantly right-handed, it would only be logical to hold the knife in the right hand and cut the left arm or hand.

Sometimes (in four spells) the blood of an animal was used, and in three of the four cases it was that of a calf. The reasoning here may have been that the animal was both innocent and valuable, although it should not necessarily be assumed that the beast was killed in the process of obtaining its blood. All three spells are intended to create a talisman – one for success in gaming, another to preserve luck, and the third for protection against evil – and in all three the stave is to be carved on special parchment or paper[40]. One spell in the Stockholm MS, to obtain a woman's love, employs snake's blood[41], and the stave is carved on the floor in the victim's path.

---

[40] One specifies the skin of a heifer, another the skin of a heifer's first calf, the third sanctified paper.

[41] As Flowers has pointed out, this may mean semen.

The sorcerer's own saliva was also fairly frequently used, usually in conjunction with a finger (see above, under 'The carving instruments'). This was often the chosen fluid when the 'carved' surface was the sorcerer's own skin, or when the magical intention was to be transmitted secretly and by direct contact[42].

Milk is used for three of the spells, but never to 'stain' a stave or any other carved sign. In one case, taken from AM 434 a 12mo 'Lækningkver', we see the instruction:

> "For pain in the eyes, write on parchment vau, nau, dele, neamon, aa-leph, gimel and anne; take three drops of milk from a woman who has a boy-child at the breast and add it to a raw egg, and let a man whom he has never seen before give it to him."

It can be seen that this spell is heavily influenced by the Western Tradition and, were it not for the inclusion of the (Hebraic) words on parchment, I might have excluded it altogether as a magical operation.

---

[42] Saliva is, in my own experience, very much under-rated. It can be used to transmit an intention at a distance. Once, in a seemingly interminable queue at Stansted Airport, I focused on the runes Fehu and Raiðo for a few seconds, absorbing them into my being. Then I wetted a finger with saliva and traced these on my palm in the form of a bindrune with the intention to 'make the queue move faster', then blew across the open palm before the saliva had dried. The queue immediately came out of deadlock, and we were soon at the service counter. I have used this operation on several occasions since, for example in traffic jams, and it invariably works.

The same, predominantly beneficent 'book of healing' also has a charm to ensure sound sleep, redolent of the less benign sleep-thorn spells in the other books:

> "If you want to make a man sleep, take milk and singed cat hair and rub them around the teeth of a sleeping man. If you want to wake him, take a chicken's egg and break it in his mouth, and he will awaken then and there."

One can only be glad not to have been the patient of this 'healer'; already sleeping, he rubs a pungent concoction of milk and singed cat's hair around your teeth, and then he wakes you up by cracking an egg into your open mouth!

Coincidentally, the last bodily excretion that we deal with – excrement or, in the vulgar parlance, shit – also crops up in a sleep spell. The Icelandic word used is *saur*, and I will use the solid, evocative, English word 'shit' in my own translation:

> "If you want a man to sleep. Take a dead man's shit or a [living] man's shit, or man's shit and ödu (now unknown Icelandic word[43]) earth, and lay in the middle of his chest, and carve these staves on a piece of baleen with steel."

––––––––––––––––––––

[43] The Icelandic dialects were eliminated by educators in the nationalist fervour of the 19th Century. My guess is that *ödu mold* is earth from a grave.

Figure 33: Staves from item 59, Lbs 2413 8vo

Herbs and vegetable preparations

Herbs are rarely used in the operations described in these grimoires. Where they are used, it is almost always in connection with scrying to identify a thief or to prevent theft. For scrying purposes, a stave was carved into the bottom of a vessel and then yarrow was ground into it as finely as possible, after which it was filled with water. The words that accompany the working and, in a couple of cases, the similarity of the staves, suggest a common origin. This scrying spell can first be found in AM 434 a 12mo 'Lækningakver' from around 1500:

> "If a man wants to know who has stolen from him, carve this sign on the bottom of a box, and grind up yarrow in the water as small as possible, and speak these words: 'I desire, by the nature of the herb and the power of the sign, that I may see the shadow of the one who has stolen from me and others.'"

Figure 34: Thief-finding stave from AM 434 a 12mo

The same spell is found, with almost identical wording, a century later in the Stockholm MS and three centuries later in Lbs 2413 8vo.

Yarrow is also used in an *Ægishjálmur*-type working to be found in 'Lækningakver', and this working will be covered in detail in chapters 9 and 10.

Instead of yarrow, another herb known in Icelandic as *friggjar gras* could be used in the aforementioned scrying operations. It is mentioned in the Stockholm MS. As Flowers points out in the notes to his translation of this book of magic, the identity of the herb is disputed, though the Cleasby-Vigfusson Icelandic-English dictionary unequivocally translates it as mandrake. The mandrake, however, is native to southern Europe and the Levant. The most likely candidate, to my mind, is *platanthera hyperborea*, the northern green orchid, which is native to Iceland.

Grape juice (*vínberjalögur*) is mentioned in one spell in Lbs 2413 8vo. Perhaps it is no coincidence that this also relates to theft:

> "If a man drives one's sheep from a pasture: carve these staves in a path he will walk and he will be stuck until you come to him. Water them with grape juice. They [i.e. the staves] come here."

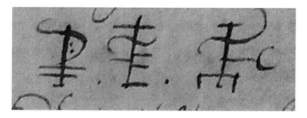

Figure 35: Staves from item 121, Lbs 2413 8vo

The climate of Iceland is not conducive to growing grapes, and it is likely that juice from some local berry is meant here. Bilberries grow profusely on Icelandic hillsides, providing food for ptarmigan and for humans. The juice of freshly crushed bilberries has a blood-red hue, and may have represented a substitute for blood to colour the staves.

Finally, a fairly complex thief-finding operation in the Stockholm MS begins:

> "If, with magical knowledge, you want to find out who is stealing from you, then take a little thorn-bush and carry it on your person so that it may not be separated from you..."

Flowers posits in a note on this spell "Probably hawthorn or sloe", but neither the hawthorn nor the blackthorn is native to Iceland. More likely, the thorny bush was one of two species of rose that grow there, *Þyrnirós* (Rosa pimpinellifolia) or *Glitrós* (Rosa dumalis).Thorns are associated with the Thurs-rune, of course, and its modern equivalent in writing is still called *þorn* in Icelandic. The spell does not elaborate further on the role of the little thorn-bush, but the rest of the text is devoted to a Thor's Hammer-type working, whereby a spike is knocked into the eye of an image to torment the thief. We will return to this working in chapter 10.

Conclusions

It would appear that Icelandic magicians usually performed their workings with anything that came to hand, and that the primacy of the stave – often in combination with an incantation – trumped all other considerations. This is entirely in accordance with the picture of magic that we get from the sagas, as in the episode where Egill Skallagrímsson carves uses his knife to carve runes on a horn of poisoned ale, stains them with his blood, and causes the horn to split asunder. Magical signs were often carved with the sorcerer's own eating-knife or scratched with an ordinary awl, but some operations might specify that they should be carved with something more specialised such as an awl of lead or silver or a copper knife. Such tools would have had no place in an ordinary household. Human bone was sometimes used for carving in spells of malign intent. All the operations specifying the use of a pen or pencil come from the relatively late grimoire Lbs 2413 8vo (c. 1800), and it is possible that the traditional custom of literal carving was passing out of fashion as more convenient pen and paper (or parchment) became more readily available.

Similar observations can be made with regard to the material that was to be carved. Leaving aside the cases where a sign was to be carved directly to the 'target' or in its proximity (on a bedpost, for example), it would seem that staves could quite often be carved on any handy material. However, this still leaves us with a considerable body of spells which stipulate a specific material, and some of these must have taken considerable trouble or expense to acquire. It cannot be imagined, for example, that one would normally have a human skull or unused silver lying around in one's farmstead. Even the materials to which one can imagine the average farmer or fisherman having some degree of access, such as a newly acquired washing bowl, the skin of a heifer's first calf, the spine of a dogfish or the carapace of a lumpfish, give an indication that some forethought was required, and that these materials were probably stored away for future magical use.

Except for the one spell calling for use of the excrement of a dead man, the auxiliary materials used seem to have been quite ordinary and readily available: some blood or saliva, and occasionally yarrow, a herb that grows quite profusely in Iceland.

The picture that emerges has two sides. On the one hand, it is mainly one of ad hoc magic, performed with everyday materials and implements, sometimes supplemented with a little blood or spit. On the other hand, it indicates that there must have been dedicated sorcerers who carefully assembled a 'toolbox' of magical materials for future use, made special tools such as copper knives and hammers, and plundered graves for bones. It is highly conceivable that such magicians lent or sold their skills to others, for it is not often in the course of normal life that one individual has resort to all of these things to right his own circumstances.

CHAPTER 6

TIME AND SPACE

Although precise timing features in only a few spells, there are some indications that it could be important. In some cases, the timing is determined in a logical and non-magical way by the purpose of the spell. For example, a spell in the Stockholm MS 'for the protection of your horse' calls for certain words in dog-Latin to be said "when you come into a troublesome situation." Similarly, an incantation against being hit by flying objects such as 'troll shot' is to be spoken immediately, presumably while adopting the sensible course of ducking and taking cover. And, of course, for oneiromantic workings one has to be asleep, so they are best done at night (although the preparation for these could be done at other times of day). On the other hand, there are examples of simple timing that cannot be explained by normal causality, such as a working (also in the Stockholm MS) to inflict fear on an enemy:

> "If you want your enemy to be afraid of you when he sees you, then carve these staves on a piece of shrub-oak and wear it in the middle of your chest, **and see to it that you see him before he sees you**."

Figure 36: Staves from item 9 of Stockholm MS

More complex instructions relating to the timing or duration of a working can be found in other spells. Dawn and sunrise were regarded as favourable times in some of them, as in the *Ægishjálmur*-type working quoted previously under 'Herbs and vegetable preparations' and this one for weather control from Lbs 2413 8vo:

> "If you want a favourable wind. Carve these staves on brass and walk in the direction that you want the wind to come from, and wave them three times in the air **when the sun is directly in the east**, and a favourable wind will come. Carve with steel."

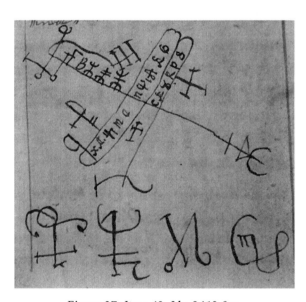

Figure 37: Item 43, Lbs 2413 8vo

High noon could also be a favourable time, as in this operation from the Stockholm MS:

> "If you wish that someone in particular should not come to your farm, carve this stave on rowan-wood **when the sun is at its zenith** and walk three times with the sun and three times widdershins around your farm, and hold the rowan-stick that the stave is carved on, together with some sharp-spined thorn-grass* and then put both of them up over the middle of your door."

*Thistle

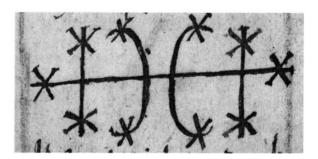

Figure 38: Item 29, Stockholm MS

Moon phases are also considered important in some workings. In general terms, the waxing moon or the full moon were favoured, there being no spells in these grimoires calling for activity under the waning moon. A certain night is stipulated in some, such as the first or third night of the moon's cycle, and the moon phase could also be combined with other factors, such as the sea's tide being at its highest as in this spell from ÍB 383 4to 'Huld':

"Thief-stave. Let this stave be carved on a wash-bowl, outside and inside, **when the moon is full and at high tide**."

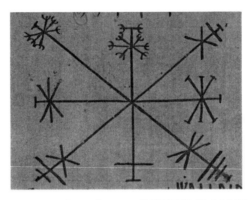

Figure 39: Stave from spell XXVIII, Huld MS

Specific days of the week are given for a few spells. In Lbs 2413 8vo, certain staves to ease the task of rowing are to be carved on the rowlocks of the boat on a Friday. This may be because of the association of Friday with fish (it being a Christian fast day, when no meat was to be eaten), or it may represent a residual connection, via Freyr and Freya, with the Vanic god Njörður, who rules coastal waters. An oneiromantic working in the same book instructs:

"Carve these staves on splintered oak [or possibly a splinter of oak] with a pencil when a **Saturday** moon is 5 nights old according to German numbers[44], and keep under your head: to dream what you will."

---

[44] This is something of a mystery. I have not been able to establish what is meant by 'German numbers' or how this count might differ

Sunday is also cited as the day to perform two other workings, both in Lbs 2413 8vo and both relating to theft. In one, to identify a thief by dreaming, staves are to be carved using an unused steel knife that was "made between daybreak and matins on a Sunday." In another, to compel the thief to return stolen goods, the working is to be performed "while the moon is one night old on a Sunday." One can put forward different arguments as to why Sunday was considered propitious. On the one hand, there is a sense in many of these magical operations of going against Christian dogma. For example, some spells also instruct "and do not say your prayers" or even to recite the Lord's Prayer backwards. Sunday has always been the compulsory day of rest in the Christian week, so the power of the working may have been derived in part from its defiance of religious custom. On the other hand, it is possible that a connection still existed with ancient Nordic lore and the significance of the Sun-rune, 'Sól' in the Icelandic Rune Poem. The Latin/Icelandic gloss that was later added to the relevant verse of the poem reads "Wheel. 'Descendant of the victorious one'". The connection of Sunday with the prospect of victory is further enhanced in the Icelandic verse, still recited today, about the days of the week:

"Sunnudagur til sigurs,
mánudagur til mæðu,
þriðjudagur til þrautar,
miðvikudagur til moldar,
fimmtudagur til frama,

---

from any other, and would be happy to hear from anyone who can shed light on this.

föstudagur til fjár,
laugardagur til lukku"

which translates as:

"Sunday for victory,
Monday for trouble,
Tuesday for trials,
Wednesday for earth,
Thursday for fame,
Friday for money,
Saturday for luck."

The decision to choose Sunday for the day of the working may therefore have been influenced by the desire to attract 'victorious' forces.

The duration of magical operations was also sometimes important, with the numbers three, six and nine having special significance. This is entirely in accordance with ancient Nordic lore, especially as regards the numbers three and nine[45]. Several oneiromantic spells require sleeping on a stave for three or six nights in order to see the face of the thief; another requires the stave to be buried under the turf of a grave for nine nights before sleeping on it. One working to magically 'load' gaming dice in 'Lækningakver' calls for a complex succession of actions over multiple periods of three

---

[45] Compare, for example, the nine worlds of Nordic cosmology, the nine nights for which Odin hung on the World Tree, and the three interlocking triangles of the Valknut.

nights – nine in total. We will return to this one later, when dealing with the matter of complexity.

Only one annual feast seems to have been regarded as especially propitious for magical operations, at least in the six books under review here, and that was the feast of St John the Baptist on 24 June. To be more precise, it was usually on the eve of the feast that the magic was to be performed, on what was known in England as (Old) Midsummer's Eve. Jacqueline Simpson and Steve Road, in "A Dictionary of English Folklore" (OUP, 2000), write:

> "Astronomically, the summer solstice is 21 June, but tradition throughout Europe reckons 24 June as Midsummer Day, and calls the night of 23/4 Midsummer Eve, Midsummer Night, or St John's Eve, since 24 June is the feast of St John the Baptist."

It seems to have been universally a time for divination and a night when the veil between the worlds of humans and the 'hidden folk' was thin, as one can see in Shakespeare's play "A Midsummer Night's Dream". Several of the divinatory workings in the Icelandic books of magic are to take place on this night.

We have already touched on the dimension of space in chapter 4, under 'The methods of delivery'. The evidence of these six grimoires seems to indicate that space was, for the most part, a matter of practical consideration in Icelandic magic. If you wanted to put someone into a charmed sleep, you had to get close enough to lay a carved stave under his head. If you wanted to seduce a girl, you could shake her hand with the staves traced in saliva on your palm, or you could carve a stave on her bedpost. A sheep rustler could be held in place by carving staves on the track that he was likely to take. (On the other hand, you could stop bleeding or inflict intolerable farting at a distance!) The list of examples goes on. What we clearly do *not* see, in most of these workings, is an instruction in the style of the Western Tradition to perform magical rites at a certain physical place as determined by correspondences: there are no injunctions to perform operations in protected circles, at crossroads, or even in 'some neglected place'. It would seem that the most a sorcerer would usually desire was his habitual abode and, perhaps, a modicum of privacy. A few spells, however, do indicate that they are to be performed in a specific physical location. Take, for example, this one from Lbs 2413 8vo:

> "Walk fasting **along the burn that runs from east to west** before a bird flies over it, and hold your hands in the water while saying your prayer. Then, using the right hand, make this cross [actually a very simple ægishjálmur] with a wet piece of curved horn between your eyes."

This spell, which is clearly of the apotropaic, helm-of-awe type, holds relatively complex instructions – by Icelandic standards – regarding place, direction, time, action, incantation, the stave to be carved, the surface to be carved and the instrument that is to be used.

Then there is the dice-loading spell, already quoted above, which calls for the secretion of dice in a churchyard and even on the altar of a Church, and the necromantic operation that calls for the burying of a stave under the turf of a grave logically requires that one should be in a graveyard.

Even though the location of the working – except for the examples just quoted – might have been irrelevant, there are tantalising glimpses of the importance of direction, especially in relation to the sun's course. Some operations are to be performed when the sun is in the east or south, but there are also spells that operate with a different orientation. A working that may be deduced to be a scrying spell, from AM 434 a 12mo 'Lækningakver', reads:

> "Take the herb called yarrow on the feast day of Bishop Jón, and **do not let the sun shine on it**, and take it with all the roots, and read these words over it **when the sun is in the centre of the southeast**, and get for yourself a cask with four hoops: Qui te creavit qui perte latronem vel furenntem."

Then there is a spell in Lbs 2413 8vo for success in wrestling, which calls on Thor and Odin, and ends "and turn your face **to the northwest**", and a whetstone spell in the Huld MS in which, after the staves have been carved, the whetstone is to be used facing away from the sun.

The dice-loading spell already mentioned twice requires the dice to be buried in the north, south and east of a churchyard, but not in the west.

Such directional indications, in terms of the points of the compass, offer contributions towards the reconstruction of forgotten Nordic lore, as do passages from the sagas such as this one from the Saga of Gisli:

"There was something else that seemed to have a strange meaning, that snow never stayed on the south-west side of Thorgrim's mound and it did not freeze there; and men explained this by saying that he must have been so favoured by Frey for his sacrifices that the god was unwilling to have frost come between them.[46]"

This passage clearly implies that Frey's quarter is to the southwest.

Circumambulation is mentioned in only one spell, and in this spell the walker moves both "three times with the sun (*réttsælis*) and three times widdershins (*rangsælis*)." On this basis, it is difficult to draw a conclusion with regard to the significance attached to these directions. However, if we diverge for a moment from the six grimoires, we find that Dillmann argues[47] that widdershins motion was intended to change the status quo and sunwise motion to reinforce it: if the weather was initially calm, a working involving widdershins motion could be used to whip up a storm, and motion in the same direction could also be used to make an existing storm abate. Conversely, sunwise movement will exacerbate a storm that is already blowing. Only further research, based on other grimoires, will confirm or deny this hypothesis.

---

[46] "Three Icelandic Outlaw Sagas", Viking Society for Northern Research 2004, pp. 30-31.
[47] Dillmann, op. cit., pp. 115-116.

Conclusions

Clearly, there were some magical operations in which the dimensions of time and space were important, where it mattered not only when and where you performed a spell, but also how often and which direction you faced. It is entirely possible that a richer lore is hidden or omitted in all the other spells which give no directions as to timing or spatial considerations, or that these factors were being forgotten as the sorcerers were progressively driven into the privacy of their own dwellings as the witchcraft persecutions gathered strength. Only diligent study of the remaining grimoires, supplemented by personal experimentation, will tell us more.

CHAPTER 7

THE PERSISTENCE OF
HEATHEN BELIEF

The issues of religion and belief in supernatural entities have already been touched on in other chapters, but let us now turn more explicitly to the evidence for a survival of Heathen belief in the spell-books of the early modern period.

At the turn of the 10th and 11th Centuries, the people of Iceland had been more or less evenly divided between adherents of the ancient Germanic faith and those of the new, Christian religion emanating from mainland Europe. It is hardly surprising that Christianity had gained such a substantial hold, even within 120 years of the first permanent settlements. Though many of the prominent men and women leading the settlement effort were Heathens from Norway, many of their thralls were drawn from the countries now known as Scotland and Ireland, which had already been converted to Christianity. The influence of the thrall class should not be underestimated, for it was in the company of thralls – nursemaids, household servants and artisans – that many a young noble would spend his or her formative years. Furthermore, those adults who wished to personally engage in economic dealings with Norway, Denmark and other countries found it increasingly convenient to adopt the new religion in order to oil the wheels of commerce.

In the end, however, it was probably the trade embargo imposed by the crusading King Olaf Tryggvason of Norway, together with his threat to invade Iceland, that was most instrumental in bringing about the official switch, by decision of the Althing, to Christianity in 1000 CE. At the start, certain accommodations were made for those who wished to continue following the old faith, but from its outset Christianity has never been a religion willing to comfortably co-exist with other religions if it can get the upper hand. As the missionaries flooded in and monasteries and episcopal residences were established, the former promises were nullified until (as we have seen) even the days of the week were being renamed to eliminate any reference to the old deities.

We will probably never know how much of this affected the lives of ordinary Icelanders in practical terms, as they lived out their days on isolated farmsteads. In common with the experience shared in many other countries, the religious regime under the Roman Catholic Church could be surprisingly accommodating of folk customs derived from the supplanted religions, as long as people paid their tithes, attended Church on Sunday and holy days, and did not go out of their way to confront the position of the See of Rome. This easy-going approach only changed when new and heretical Christian teachings started to challenge the dominance of the Roman Catholic Church. It is therefore entirely possible that some people quietly continued to privately acknowledge their favourite gods among the old pantheon, along with the elves inhabiting rocks, valleys, ponds and copses, even as they mumbled their prayers in tribute to the half-understood mysteries of the imported religion.

Figure 40: Signpost to Álfatjörn (Elf-pond) near Hólmavík (Author's own photograph)

The full force of the Inquisition – which was directed, *nota bene*, against heresy rather than against residual pagan beliefs – never hit Iceland, probably because this isolated community was something of a political irrelevance compared to powerful bishoprics and principalities in mainland Europe. The conversion of Denmark to Lutheranism, and the subsequent forcible conversion of Iceland to the same faith – resulting in a civil war – was another kettle of fish. This brought new and uncompromising attitudes towards the relationship between mortals and the Kingdom of Heaven, and woe betide anyone who strayed from its puritanical path. It was at this point, from the mid-sixteenth century until the end of the seventeenth century, that every effort was made to extirpate not only malevolent witchcraft, but also such folk-magic and beliefs in the elder gods as may have survived. It was in this atmosphere that some of our primary sources were written, and it is a wonder that any of them have been passed down to us today.

The gods and goddesses of the old Germanic pantheon certainly survived in the magic of early modern Iceland, albeit in a small minority of spells. In some cases they are called upon together with the Biblical demons Satan and Beelzebub, in others (without any apparent sense of irony) together with Christ, the Holy Trinity and the Virgin Mary, and there are even spells in which Heathen deities are called upon together with both sides of the conflicting Biblical forces. However, there are also spells in which only the northern deities are evoked. Odin is mentioned most often; understandably, as he is depicted as the prime god of magic in the Poetic Edda.

As well as being evoked under his prime name *Óðinn*, cognate with Woden – 'the raging one' – he is called upon using the bynames *Fjölnir*[48] and *Hliðskjálfargramur*[49]. With five mentions, Thor is the next most frequently evoked of the elder gods, closely followed by Baldur (mentioned in four

---

[48] Appears in the Grimnismál (Poetic Edda).
[49] Appears as a kenning for Odin in the Skaldskaparmál (Prose Edda).

spells). Other familiar gods and goddesses named among the magical workings are Tyr, Loki, Hænir, Frigg, Freya, Freyr, Njord and Gefun (Gefjon). In addition, there are more shadowy figures – most of them mentioned in a single spell in Lbs 2413 8vo – some of whom are hard to identify. There is the elusive star-hero Örvandill, mentioned only once in Norse mythology[50], who may be cognate with the Old English Earandel; then there are Jöfrir, Þórir, Þumill, Hringsþornir, Ölver, Illi, Birgir and Gusta. Some of these may be kennings for the known gods of the pantheon. Jöfrir, for example, may be derived from 'jöfurr', a wild boar, and hence a kenning for Freyr.

There are also tangential references to the Heathen deities in two other spells. *Friggjar gras* (Frigg's herb) has already been mentioned in connection with the use of herbs and other vegetable preparations, and item number XVI in the Huld MS refers to the Hammer of Thor, "which magicians used to summon thieves and for diverse works of magic." (See chapter 10 for more on this subject.)

Despite the efforts of the Church to demonise the pre-Christian pantheon, the evidence shows that the old gods were not only called upon for workings of malign intent. They were also evoked for thief-finding, for success in gaming and wrestling, to soothe anger and for all-round protection. Although it is not possible to extract direct

---

[50] The Skaldskaparmál relates that Thor rescued Örvandill (or Aurvandil) from Jötunheim and carried him away in a basket. As they travelled between the worlds, one of the hero's toes protruded from the basket and froze, whereupon Thor broke it off and cast it into the heavens to become a star.

correlations between the purpose of the working and the deity evoked, the very fact that they *were* evoked – often with great passion, to judge from the wording – shows that the elder gods and goddesses lived on in the hearts and minds of the sorcerers of this era.

CHAPTER 8

RUNES, CIPHERS AND SECRECY

For those of us who have already expended a great deal of effort in mastering 'Rune Magic', the magical practices of early modern Iceland can present a confusing and even disappointing picture. The modern 'tradition' of northern magic, heavily influenced by Guido von List and subsequently refined by other great writers (not least the Rune Gild's present Yrmin-Drighten, Edred Thorsson), places great emphasis on the 24 runes of the Elder Futhark and the 16 runes of the Younger Futhark, and on their practical manipulation to achieve personal growth and operative effects in the external world. So, we may ask, where are the Futhark runes in these Icelandic grimoires? There are magical signs and images (*galdrastafir* and *galdramyndir*) a-plenty, but there is very little that we can recognise – even as bindrunes – as being derived from our familiar Futhark rows. Even the *fretrúnir* used in the spells to inflict farting on a victim do not follow the usual patterns (see chapter 4, figure 12).

In 2008, after my first visit to Iceland and, in particular, the Icelandic Museum of Sorcery and Witchcraft in Hólmavík, I wrote this rather dismissive comment in my diary:

"By this time, the runic tradition had become highly fragmented and debased, but it was still obviously present in a form of sorcery seen nowhere else in that era."

In retrospect, this was a very arrogant and ignorant statement.

By around 1500 CE, the Icelandic rune-row had expanded again from the 16 characters of the Old Icelandic Rune Poem to incorporate and assimilate the new letters and sounds that had come with the general adoption of the Roman alphabet. As in other alphabets (such as Hebrew) a system of dots was used to make distinctions between similar but distinct consonants such as 'B' and 'P', and 'K' and 'G'. Accommodations were also made for differences in the pronunciation of vowels and diphthongs. There was no standardisation, but in general, the rune-row came to look something like this:

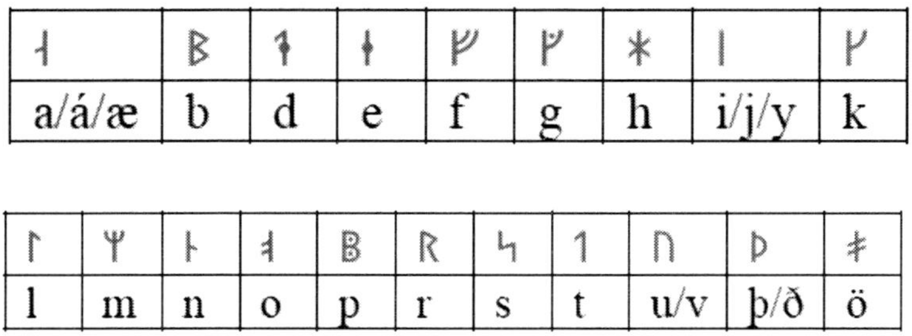

ᛆ	ᛒ	ᛑ	ᛂ	ᛔ	ᚹ	ᚼ	ᛁ	ᚴ
a/á/æ	b	d	e	f	g	h	i/j/y	k

ᛚ	ᛘ	ᚿ	ᚮ	ᛔ	ᚱ	ᛌ	ᛐ	ᚢ	ᚦ	ᛪ
l	m	n	o	p	r	s	t	u/v	þ/ð	ö

Figure 41: Later Icelandic runes

This was far from the only rune-row, however. Many of them are recorded, primarily by later antiquarians who presumably had access to manuscripts now lost or ignored. One of the best sources for these, to my knowledge, is

Jochum Eggertsson (1896-1966) who, writing under the nom-de-plume 'Skuggi', published the book 'Galdraskræða' (Book of Magic) in 1940[51]. The book contains many different rune-rows, together with glosses for some of the runes, plus many spells drawn from earlier manuscripts. In the 1940 edition, everything was rendered in his own handwriting and all the staves were also painstakingly drawn by hand.

The only manuscript among those presently under consideration to systematically list a variety of rune-rows and ciphers is the Huld manuscript (ÍB 383 4to) which was compiled by the antiquarian Geir Vigfússon in the 1860s. The Huld MS gives no less than 38 pages of runes and ciphers, including *málrunir* (speech-runes) and *villuletur* (delusion-script, or possibly heretical script). As one can see from Figure 42 below, there were many possible runic 'alphabets', and they only partly resemble the Migration-age and Viking-age runes so familiar to modern Rune-magicians. It seems fairly safe to assume that each sorcerer developed his own, secret runes and perhaps passed them on to favoured apprentices.

---

[51] This was republished in a different format by the Icelandic publishing house Lesstofan in 2013. The present editor and presenter of the book intends to bring out an English-language edition soon. Jochum Eggertson's contribution falls outside the scope of this present work and is worthy of further study in its own right.

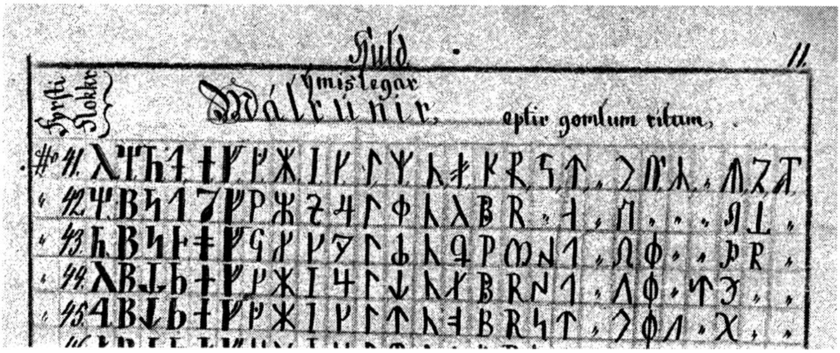

Figure 42: Speech-runes in Huld MS

The grimoire listed as Lbs 764 8vo – the second part of "Tvær Galdraskræður" – was largely written in a cipher (to which I presently have no access), and respect is due to the diligence of those who interpreted it.

The second part of the Huld MS, in which 30 separate spells are listed, makes frequent use of both runic characters and ciphered Roman letters. Fortunately, with some knowledge of runes and of the Icelandic language, these are not very hard to decipher. The only bugbear is that the use of runes and of the ciphers in 'modern' letters can vary from spell to spell, and does not match exactly with the lists provided in the first part of the manuscript, so some flexibility and lateral thinking is required. The likely explanation for this is that Geir Vigfússon, being an antiquarian rather than a magician, compiled the lists of runes and ciphers as a separate exercise from the reproduction of the spells depicted in the latter half of his manuscript, and made no attempt to achieve any forced consistency.

It is certain that the power of purely runic characters was used in some of the spells. The fart-runes have already been referred to in this and other chapters (because they have many fascinating aspects, and not only for their humorous value), but there are other spells which employ only runic characters as opposed to the more pictorial staves and images. Take, for example, the gambling spell in AM 434 a 12mo 'Lækningakver', in which the following staves must be carved on a stick or sheet of paper and laid under the gambling table:

Figure 43: 'Gambling' runes from AM 434 a 12mo. They read "Olafr:Olafr:Haralldr:Haralldr:Eirikr".

Or these, from the Stockholm MS, for protection against all kinds of evil:

Figure 44: Item 18 from Stockholm MS

Or these more complex runes, again from the Stockholm MS, to inflict vomiting:

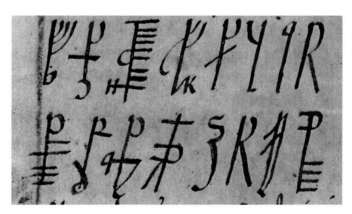

Figure 45: Item 27 from Stockholm MS

Furthermore, there are oblique references to the runes of the Elder Futhark in the names of certain magical staves. The *augnaþurs* (eye-Thurs) has already been mentioned in chapter 4, and this makes reference to the third stave of all the classic Futhark rows: the Thurs-rune. Then there is

'Hagall', or hail, the ninth rune in the Elder Futhark and the seventh in the younger Futhark, reflected in this stave from Lbs 2413 8vo:

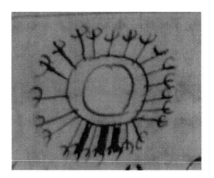

Figure 46: The 'greater Hagall'

The final spell listed in Lbs 2413 8vo, a working to ensure that a girl never marries (the wording of the main text implies that she should love only the sorcerer) also makes reference to runes, beginning "Write the following verse on grey calf-skin ..." and ending "...and write in speech-runes."

So what are we to make of all this? Even though the forms of the runic characters may differ from the older Futhark rows, and though the number of spells purely employing runic characters and no other magical images may be few in number, it is clear that runes were used in some cases as the vehicles for magical intent. The glosses (*kenningar*) provided by Jochum Eggertsson for eight rows of speech-runes also indicate that a considerable body of runelore existed, in addition to the lore we can cull from the three main rune poems[52]. When we look at the Huld MS, on the other hand, the runic characters are not used as the magical vehicles but rather to provide part of the instructions for the use of another magic sign. Their purpose was to maintain secrecy and hide the meaning of the instructions from the uninitiated, as one can see from the image below.

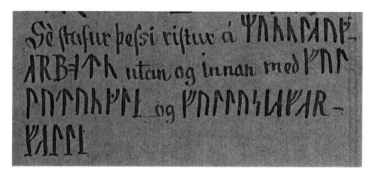

Figure 47: From Huld MS; "Let this stave be carved on the bottom of a wash-bowl, outside and inside, at the full moon and at high tide."

The use of other scripts and ciphers (some of them numerical) in addition to the runes tends to indicate that secrecy was a primary concern of magicians. This cannot be explained merely in terms of self-protection from the authorities: during the witchcraft persecution of the seventeenth century, possession of a book in a secret script would have added to the weight of the case against the defendant rather than detracted from it. There must have been other reasons. One motivation for using secret scripts was undoubtedly a desire to hide the spell's instructions

---

[52] The Old Icelandic Rune Poem, the Old Norse Rune Rhyme and the Old English Rune Poem.

from the prying eyes of other people who were not magicians, and perhaps also from other, competing magicians, but it is arguable that the secrecy in itself was considered a powerful factor in enhancing the potency of a working.

This brings us to an important issue in the general debate concerning magic in our post-Enlightenment, 'scientific' world. There are rationalists who argue that, in order for a magical spell to take effect, the victim (or beneficiary) must necessarily be aware of its casting; the effect, they argue, is then brought about purely by psychological effects. The victim of a curse descends into despair, makes poor judgements and thereby brings about his own downfall; conversely, the beneficiary of a 'lucky' or protective charm is buoyed by optimism and, feeling free of care, waxes in health and well-being. Others, maintaining a more open mind regarding the effectiveness of magical operations – even if they are not practising magicians themselves – will allow for the possibility of a working taking effect even when the target is entirely unaware of it. This debate finds its way even into academic studies of mediaeval magic and witchcraft, making the author's standpoint apparent even as he studiously tries to avoid it. Stephen A. Mitchell, for example, writes:

> "Another important component in this case [of Ragnhildr tregagás of Bergen, Norway] is the degree to which the declaration of the curse must be public – very public, in fact. Indeed, it is worth repeating the sequence of events here: on the first night of the wedding, Ragnhildr carries out the three fundamental aspects of the curse – hiding the

objects in the bed, uttering the actual curse formula, and spitting on Bárðr – but it is as if these actions are not operational until she makes her public declaration of the curse. Thus Ragnhildr, the perpetrator of the charm, finds it necessary to go up to her rival at the wedding feast and declare openly that she has made her erstwhile lover impotent – the possibility of revenge from Bárðr and his party, or of accusation from the authorities, seems not to be a consideration for her, so critical an element to the success of the charm does broadcasting the news seem to be. Performance matters, and it is obvious that how things are done is nowhere of greater relevance than in the context of highly prescribed ritualized behaviour of the sort one associates with casting a spell.[53]"

Without overtly saying so, Mitchell implicitly argues here that the spell's main, indeed only effect is exerted by the public declaration.

Kieckhefer appears to take a different point of view in the following passage:

"Because these curses would be uttered in secrecy, the victim would have little reason to know what they were or even that they had been uttered, and for that reason they probably show up in court records much less often than they were actually used. For different but equally obvious reasons the

---

[53] Stephen A. Mitchell, "Witchcraft and Magic in the Nordic Middle Ages", University of Pennsylvania Press, Philadelphia 2011, p. 72.

victims of sorcery could not present as evidence potions that had been consumed. What the accusers did have to show the judges were magical amulets that had been left under their thresholds or beds to do them harm.[54]"

Neither Mitchell nor Kieckhefer give much attention to Iceland in their respective works, Mitchell focusing primarily on mainland Scandinavia and Kieckhefer on the German states of mediaeval Europe. The evidence from the Icelandic grimoires is that secrecy was highly important and that the victim should usually be kept unaware of the working directed against him or her. In addition to the many spells implicitly calling for secrecy ("carve on bedpost", "place under head of sleeping man", "place the staves under the bed cover" etc.), there are several that explicitly state that the victim should be unaware (*honum óvitandi*) or that nobody should know what you have done (*svo ei viti*). There is no mention in these of any subsequent declaration, to the individual in question or in public, of having performed the magical operation. This completely contradicts the claims of rationalists that it is necessary for the target to know that magic has been performed, whether malicious or benign.

Conclusions

Runic characters were certainly in use in early modern Iceland, albeit not always in a form immediately recognisable to those familiar with the Elder and Younger

---

[54] Kieckhefer, op. cit., p. 82.

Futhark rows. The actual sequence of the runes and their division into 3 *ættir* seems to have become neglected; even the earliest grimoire in this collection appends a rune-row almost as an afterthought, but in the order of the Roman alphabet. Nevertheless, it is clear from several spells that runes were used for their power in operative magic and may have been used to an even greater extent to obfuscate the meaning of instructions. In magical operations, secrecy was usually of the essence, and pains were taken to maintain it. In the grimoires too, efforts were made to conserve secrecy by the use of secret ciphers and runic characters. It is possible that the intriguing magical staves, so often employed, are themselves derived from the Futhark runes, and this possibility will be discussed in a later chapter. In the pre-literate 'Viking' era, the knowledge of the runic characters, let alone their magical power, was probably the preserve of a few. As the Roman alphabet became commonplace among the literate, to an extent that the rune-rows never had been, the knowledge and use of runes became the prerogative of an even smaller number of people who wished to conserve the old lore and use it for magical purposes.

CHAPTER 9

SOME PROMINENT THEMES AND THEIR APPLICATIONS

Having covered so many aspects of Icelandic magic in general terms – the beliefs, the purposes, the techniques, the tools, the timing and the location – it is now time to immerse ourselves in a select number of recurring intentions and the individual spells relating to them. Where possible, they will be chosen for their applicability and practicability in the present day. This should not be too difficult, for many of the preoccupations of magic are of eternal significance.

Ægishjálmur

No modern study of Icelandic magic would be complete without detailed consideration of the *ægishjálmur*, if only for the reason that it is the best known of all the staves, and that many readers would feel somewhat cheated were it not to be discussed. The contemporary fascination with this symbol most likely owes less to its purpose (for there are other spells that fulfil the same need) than to the visual attractiveness of its radial symmetry, and the fact that it has been widely employed as a touristic icon. Nonetheless, it was indeed an important symbol and magical operation, and those who employ it as a bodily adornment or an 'attention grabber' on a web page heading may at least come away with some idea of its real significance[55].

The etymology of the word is unsure, and it has been interpreted variously as 'helm of awe', 'helm of Ægir[56]', 'helm of terror', 'helm of fear' and 'cloak of awe'. In an end note to his translation of the Stockholm MS[57], Dr Stephen E. Flowers argues that its original meaning may have been a covering of the entire body rather than a helmet. This may be an important factor when considering how the stave is to be perceived when performing the working. For present purposes I will use the term 'helm of awe', as the title generally fits the bill in terms of its intention: to protect and to command respect.

The concept of the helm of awe is very old. The first known mention of it is in connection with the story of Sigurd the dragon-slayer, which probably dates back to the migration era (ca. 350-600 CE). In the Fafnismál of the Poetic Edda, Fafnir says to Sigurd:

> "With the Helm of Fear I affrighted men
> while I lay on the hated hoard;
> for the might of all men a match I weened me,
> nor e'er worthy foeman found."

To which Sigurd replies:

---

[55] Although they may be disappointed to discover that they have it as a permanent tattoo on entirely the wrong part of the body.
[56] After Ægir, the Etin who rules the deep ocean.
[57] Flowers, op. cit., note 11 to Part Two.

"The Helm of Fear hideth no one,
when bold men bare their swords;
when many are met to match their strength,
'twill be found that foremost is no one.[58]"

The import of these lines is clear: the wearing of the helm of awe can frighten and bluff, giving the impression that the wearer is 'foremost' among men, but once the real fighting has broken out the spell is broken, and one can no longer rely on the bluff.

The name 'helm of awe' would imply a physical object, but the following examples of workings from the Icelandic grimoires will show that this was anything but the case. No actual helmet is required nor, in most cases, is any visible representation of it called for. Indeed, if one's purpose is to bluff rather than start a fight, discretion is the prime requirement.

Let us look first at a spell from the oldest of the grimoires in this study, 'Lækningakver' from around 1500 CE. No drawn stave is associated with this spell, but the connections will be apparent (in all the examples below, the relevant sections are highlighted in bold, for emphasis):

"Wash yourself in water three times and read the Lord's Prayer in between, and say this three times:
'I wash from me my enemies' hatred,
the greed and wrath of powerful men,
that they may happily come to meet me

---

[58] The Poetic Edda, translation by Lee M. Hollander, University of Texas Press 1962.

and look me in the eyes laughing.
I strike love with my hand,
I put an end to lawsuits for money,
I put an end to prosecution for money,
I put an end to the persecutions of the strongest men.
May God always look upon me, and good men,
may they always see on me with joyful eyes
the Helm of Awe that I bear between my brows,
when I strive against notable men.
May everyone in the world serve me in friendship.'

Hold water in the hollows of your cupped hands."

Then compare this one from the Stockholm MS, written about a century later:

> "**I wash away from me my enemies and the robbery and wrath of powerful men,** so that they may now approach me with good cheer and look me in my eyes laughingly. I strike affection with my hand, I discharge money-fines, I discharge accusations of the most powerful men, let God see me, let every man look upon me with eyes of bliss, **I bear the helm of awe between my brows,** may the world and the land be gracious to me with regard to friends.
>
> Read this three times down into your cupped hands and have water in your hands the whole time and read a Pater Noster each time."

Bearing in mind that these are translations, from two different translators, of spells in two separate grimoires, the wording is astonishingly similar. The situation here is one of a victim, an underling, someone who is friendless and seriously in trouble. He has debts and is being pursued for them. He needs to put an end to these lawsuits and gain the love and respect of his peers and especially of the men who are more powerful than he. The method is a combination of ritual washing, incantation and visualisation. The magician takes water in his cupped hands and ritually washes all enmity from him. As he does so, he thrice makes an incantation that is a combination of appeal to a higher power (the Lord's Prayer) and an assertion of his own will (the words given above). In addition, he visualises and asserts that he bears the helm of awe between his brows (i.e. in the lower centre of the forehead, between the eyebrows). The Stockholm MS gives yet another helm-of-awe spell with very similar wording and procedures.

In the above spells, the shape of the helm of awe is not given; it is mentioned, but the assumption seems to be that the magician knows it already. However, a different spell in 'Lækningakver' has a very similar purpose and includes the depiction of a stave. It goes as follows:

> "**If you want to avoid a ruler's anger**, go out before sunrise and speak with no man going home or at home, and take the herb called yarrow and make your blood flow and sprinkle it all over the herb, and then draw this cross **on your forehead** with the herb, and thus go before your lord."

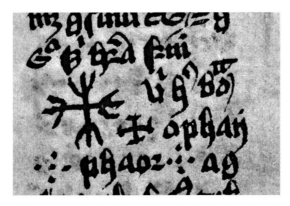

Figure 48: Simple helm-of-awe in 'Lækningakver'

The actual name 'helm of awe' is not mentioned, but it can be seen that the aim is much the same. Similar procedures can be seen in a spell recorded around 1800 in Lbs 2413 8vo, though the scribe neither mentions the helm of awe by name nor states the purpose of the working:

> "Walk fasting along the burn that runs from east to west before a bird flies over it and hold your hands in the water while saying your prayer. Then, using your right hand, make this cross with a wet piece of bent horn **between your eyes**."

(the 'cross' takes the same form as in Figure 48 above.)

The sign is referred to as a 'cross', but it is clearly a simpler form of the helm of awe. The stave could, in fact, take a variety of shapes, as shown in another item contained in the same grimoire:

"These are the nine Helms of Awe that no-one who will handle knowledge should be without, and each one should be used 99 times."

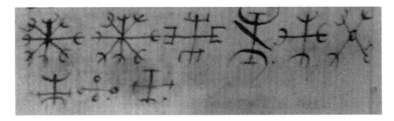

Figure 49: Item 114, Lbs 2413 8vo

Note the recurrence of the number nine here, always considered a powerful number in Nordic magic. Yet another form occurs among the later entries in the Stockholm MS:

"**To calm all anger**, make this stave on your forehead with the index finger of your left hand and say: It is the **helm of awe** which I bear **between my eyes**. Let the anger melt, let the strife stop. May every man rejoice in me as Mary rejoiced in her blessed son when she found him on the victory-rock. In the name of the father and son and holy spirit.

Figure 50: Item 41, Stockholm MS

And read:

> Ölver, Óðinn, Illi,
> everything may your will bewilder.
> May God himself with mastery,
> send love between us."

The most striking and beautiful form of the helm of awe, and the one most people associate with the term, is this one found in Lbs 143 8vo 'Galdrakver' from around 1670:

> "Ægis hjálmur. It shall be made in lead, and **when a man expects his enemies** he shall imprint it **on his forehead**. And thou wilt conquer him. It is as follows."

Figure 51: Helm of Awe from Lbs 143 8vo 'Galdrakver'

Again, the purpose of the working is that one may prevail over enemies, but this time by conquering them rather than by gaining their affection. No other actions or words are prescribed in this case and, unlike the first two spells given above, the stave is not visualised but stamped in lead and then pressed against the forehead to leave a visible mark, in much the same way that children often play with coins. One can only speculate whether the imprint was intended to be visible to the enemies or hidden under headgear.

In addition to overawing enemies and powerful persons, or gaining their goodwill, the symbol could be used for other purposes. The Stockholm MS records its use for two very different aims, as well as the workings quoted previously:

> "One should clip or cut these helms of awe onto one's livestock if they get swooning or pestilence, and the first one should be put on the left shoulder and the other one on the right.

> Likewise, while fasting, make the latter (helm of awe) with your spittle in your palm when you greet the girl whom you want to have. It should be in your right hand."

(See chapter 5, Figure 26)

The use of staves of the same (or similar) form to cure livestock is seen again in Lbs 2413 8vo. The spell quoted above, beginning *"Walk fasting along the burn…"*, continues:

"Also, clip it against evil incantations over the heart of livestock, and all these."

"All these" refers to other staves of the helm-of-awe type.

They recur in another spell of the same grimoire, item 132, with a similar purpose:

"Against misfortune to a cow or horse: clip these staves on the horse."

Strangely, the very same grimoire also employs identical staves to cast evil magic on livestock:

"If you want to cast evil magic on a sheep or a horse, clip these staves on the swirl over the heart."

It is odd that the same stave is used for different and even contradictory aims, and that the same, primary aim can apparently be achieved using different forms of the helm of awe. However, this kind of vagary is seen time and again throughout the spell books in respect of other signs and intentions. It must be remembered that the keeping of a grimoire did not necessarily make for a competent magician, that errors of transcription probably crept in over the centuries (as they certainly did in monastic texts), and that spells from older grimoires may have been copied down with a certain lack of discernment.

The majority of the intentions given above reveal a number of prime factors when it comes to the helm of awe. Firstly, it is the working of a friendless underling, a 'Billy no-mates' if you like, who is oppressed by powerful men and possibly pursued for bad debts. Secondly, it is often associated with ritual washing to wash away the anger and enmity of these powerful men. Thirdly, the sorcerer aims to gain general popularity. Finally, in such workings, the stave should always be traced or projected (by visualisation) on the forehead "between the brows". One should by no means think ill of anyone who uses the working to escape this unenviable position; after all, magic is frequently (though not exclusively) the resort of those lacking the physical or financial means to achieve their aims. On the other hand, it does not tie in well with any modern use of the symbol (e.g. as a tattoo) in an attempt to project a 'tough guy' image, and bearing it on any part of the body other than the forehead is, frankly, meaningless.

Having said this, the *ægishjálmur* is a powerful working that should form part of the stock-in-trade of any practising magician in the northern tradition. We all encounter, from time to time, situations in which we may feel overawed by others: an interview for a coveted job; a meeting with a bank manager to discuss a loan; a visit from representatives of the tax and revenue service; or perhaps suddenly being confronted with a hostile situation.

The complex and beautiful sign shown in the 'Galdrakver' of 1670 may perhaps be the most powerful, but if you are not proficient in visualisation it may be better to use the simplest form, viz: Then, when meeting an adversary, visualise the stave between your brows. Speak calmly and with authority, and let the stave do the work. It can also be visualised instantly if there has been no time to prepare in advance.

Kaupaloki – the bargain sealer

Commerce has been a constant preoccupation of mankind from the earliest times, when one person traded a store of grain for some dried fish or for a tool that had been crafted by someone else. Nowadays, it fills our lives, and fortunately all kinds of laws and regulations have been introduced to ensure fair trading… but one can never be sure. How can we be sure that the other party will fulfil their side of the deal? How can we be sure that the goods or services will arrive as promised, and be of the promised quality? We can be sure that such concerns also occupied the thoughts of Icelanders in the early modern period, for there are numerous spells designed to ensure at least a fair deal and, occasionally, advantage in the transaction. The occurrence of spells for trading reveals something of the interests of the respective scribes, for unless we count one instance in 'Lækningakver' (ca. 1500) 'against tricks', all of them are contained within the Huld MS or in the larger Lbs 2413 8vo. It is to these that we can look when seeking magical support in trading of any kind.

One of the magical concepts in trading was the *kaupaloki* or bargain-sealer. The purpose of this working is to ensure that both parties to the bargain stick to their word and deliver the goods or services as promised. The term appears twice in the Huld MS of the 1860s and once in the earlier manuscript Lbs 2413 8vo of 1800. They are reproduced below.

From Lbs 2413 8vo:

"These staves are called bargain sealers. Carve one in each palm with saliva and finger when trading with someone."

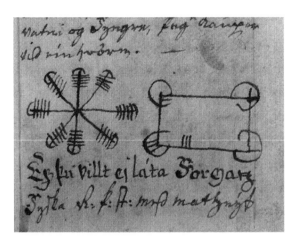

Figure 52: Bargain-sealers from Lbs 2413 8vo

From the Huld MS (no. III):

"Bargain-sealer. Score this stave on a tablet of beech wood and bear it in the centre of your chest when you want to have victory in buying and selling."

Figure 53: Bargain-sealer, no. III in Huld MS

Also from the Huld MS (no. V)

> "Bargain-sealer. Carve this stave on a tablet of beech wood and bear it in the centre of your chest."

Figure 54: Bargain-sealer, item number V from Huld MS

Note that the first set of staves is to be used immediately before one expects to close a trade deal, while the other two are talismans to be worn for steady success in buying and selling. Lbs 2413 8vo gives several other staves that have exactly the same purpose, plus one which is to gain not just a fair deal but a distinct advantage:

> "To have victory in trading. Keep this stave in your hand."

Figure 55: Item 32, Lbs 2413 8vo

This is quite an easy stave to memorise, and may therefore be discreetly traced on the palm with saliva when negotiating a bargain if you have not already prepared a talisman. Obviously, you must also have a clear idea of the terms on which you want to sell or buy. In modern commerce, there is remarkably little leeway for negotiation in everyday purchasing: most items have fixed prices and terms of delivery. However, the bigger the deal, the more negotiation is generally involved. Such staves could therefore be very useful for business people. The one 'big deal' that most of us have to negotiate at least once in our lives is the purchase of a home, and anyone who has done this will tell you that it can be a stressful and labyrinthine process. Try using these staves when you do so, having them in your hand or worn as a talisman even when you correspond in writing and certainly when you physically shake hands to seal the agreement.

'Love' spells

There are two spells in the Stockholm MS designed to win the love of a girl or woman (one of them has been mentioned previously because it employs the helm of awe), but it is to Lbs 2413 8vo that we must look for a wide range of options. The scribe who compiled this grimoire seems to have set out to make a collection of them, for most are listed in the same section of the book. As we have seen in chapter 4, there are various methods by which the intention can be delivered to the object of one's desire, and the selection below will give some idea of these.

The simplest method, if one has at least some degree of familiarity with the girl, is to transmit your intention and the power of the stave through contact by shaking hands:

> "That a girl will love you. Carve this stave in the palm of your hand with your saliva and then shake her hand[59]."

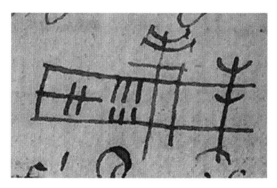

Figure 56: Item 22, Lbs 2413 8vo

If you are even more familiar, you can use your finger to trace other staves, using a finger, onto her palm rather than yours, as instructed here:

---

[59] The actual wording is "… *og heilsa henni svo*" – "and greet her thus." The handshake is assumed.

"To get a girl. Carve in her palm with your finger and say: Morsa Orsa Dorsa."

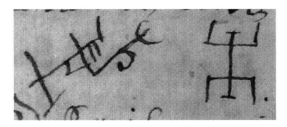

Figure 57: Item 13, Lbs 2413 8vo

As I have remarked before, if the girl is already willing to let you trace these staves on her open palm, she is probably fairly open to your advances in any case! If neither of the above opportunities presents itself, or if the love-struck swain is too shy to try them, he can always offer her a sandwich:

"That a girl will love you. Carve this stave on cheese or bread with your eating knife and give [it] to her to eat (have strong faith)."

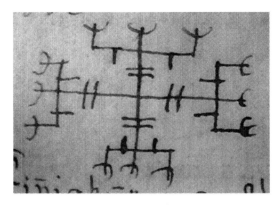

Figure 58: Item 14, Lbs 2413 8vo

In this case, the magician's will (which, it is emphasised, should be strong) is transferred in augmented form via the stave to the food, which is then ingested by the girl and absorbed. If direct contact and ingestion are ruled out, he can bring the magical staves into her proximity. There are several options here, but assuming he has access to her bed chamber he could use this working:

> "If you want a girl to love you. Carve these staves on her bedpost with steel."

Figure 59: Item 24, Lbs 2413 8vo

In this case, the staves exert a field of force in their immediate proximity, transmitting the will of the sorcerer to the target while she is asleep and, one may assume, in a receptive state. There is one spell in Lbs 2413 8vo that specifies neither contact nor proximity, stating simply:

> "To get a girl. Carve this stave in your palm with your finger and your blood."

Figure 60: Item 12, Lbs 2413 8vo

It is possible that this operation was meant to work at a distance, but it is also possible that it was another one to be transmitted by a hand-shake, and that the scribe had omitted some of the instructions.

Finally, if you feel that a more elaborate procedure would be more efficacious, are determined that the girl will marry no-one else, and are prepared to overtly show your hand, you could try this one:

> "To let a girl never marry. Write the following verse on grey calfskin and let it lie before her, but beware that no other man or woman hear or see it. Take first a lock of hair from her head and burn it on steel, then take the ash and some blood drawn from the centre of your chest, make ink of it and put it into the skull of a raven. From that, write these words: I order you, by all kinds of powers, that you will love me more than all the bloody injuries of Jesus Christ, son of God and the Virgin Mary, that you love me in this world, that you will not be at peace nor thrive unless you love me as much as

your own life, so shall you feel in your own bones that your flesh is burning. May it be so and stand as firmly as the earth stood firm because of the word of God in the name of the Father and of the Son and of the Holy Spirit, and write in speech-runes."

Here we have one of the few instances of sympathetic magic in Icelandic magic, in that something intimately connected with the target (her hair) is burned to ash and then mixed with the magician's own blood to make ink, thereby establishing a psychic link even before the words have been penned. The significance of burning the hair on steel is obscure; it could represent the 'iron will' of the magician, or it may be intended to ward off interference by any magic designed to thwart the spell. Similarly, one can only speculate as to why a raven's skull should be used as the ink pot – it may denote a connection with Odin, who is a famous seducer according to the myths. The element of ruthless compulsion – employing threats – plus the open act of placing the written spell directly in front of the victim is strongly reminiscent of Skírnir's ultimatum to Gerð after his wooing (on Frey's behalf) and offers of gifts had been refused.

If you are really considering trying any of these 'love' spells, do bear in mind that you are interfering with the free will of another person and, furthermore, that you will have to live with the consequences if the object of your desire turns out not to be as originally perceived. They bind the perpetrator as much as they bind the victim, and an amorous heart is rarely a wise counsellor.

Disputes and Lawsuits

Respect for the law has always been strong in Iceland, although its mechanisms could grind exceedingly slowly in the past, owing to the distances Sheriffs had to travel across rough terrain between scattered settlements. Such respect was very necessary, for the sagas show that disputes between neighbours were frequent, and there is no reason to believe that anything had changed in this respect by the early modern period, even if their resolution was rather less bloody than it had been in the past. Some magical assistance could therefore be a boon when defending one's case, especially for those lacking power and influence. This category of magical operations is also very relevant today as society becomes ever more litigious.

Of course, it is always wise to try to resolve disputes before lawyers get the opportunity to gleefully seize upon them and rack up the bills. In disputes between family members or other co-habitants – a husband and wife contemplating divorce, for example, or siblings quarrelling about the settlement of a will – this spell from AM 434 a 12mo 'Lækningakver' may prove sufficiently reasonable in its operation and opportune in its method:

> "If someone hates you, then take this writing and lay it under him as he sleeps, and you two will reach a settlement."

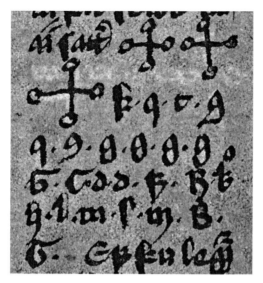

*Figure 61: Staves and letters from AM 434 12mo; three crosses,
terminating in circles, plus the letters þ.q.c.g.q.C
(reversed).g.g.g.g.G.C.d.d.f.R.k.h.l.m.s.m.B.T.*

Alternatively, you could use this one from ÍB 383 4to
'Huld':

"Reconciliation-gift.
If someone else hates you, then write these staves on
vellum and lay them under his head without him
knowing."

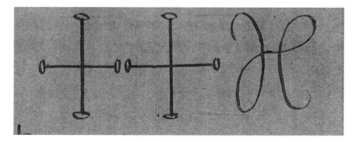

Figure 62:item number XXIV from Huld MS

Both these spells assume that the magician has access to the other party as he or she sleeps, which is why they are most useful for people sharing the same dwelling. If there is no opportunity to gain such access, this one may prove useful in bringing your opponent round to your point of view:

> "If you want to change the views of someone you have a dispute with, carve this stave on the skin of a heifer's first calf and carry it on your breast."

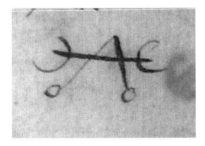

Figure 63: Item 102, Lbs 2413 8vo

If no reconciliation is possible, and the case comes to court or external arbitration, there are other staves and procedures that may be used, such as these from Lbs 2413 8vo:

> "Make this stave on yourself under your left arm, and you will win in disputes."

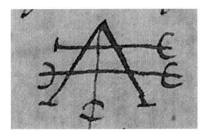

Figure 64: Item 52, Lbs 2413 8vo

"If you want to win in disputes, make these staves in your palm with your saliva and say: I wash myself in dew and daily washing water."

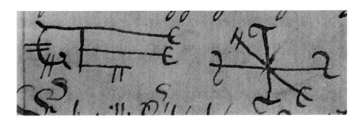

Figure 65: Item 53, Lbs 2413 8vo

Note that the words to be said are reminiscent of the Ægishjálmur-type washing rituals; there may be a connection here, as the helm-of-awe) workings also enable the user to deport himself well and without fear when facing powerful men (such as a judge).

If you are likely to see your adversary, in court or elsewhere, these staves from Lbs 764 8vo, and the words that accompany them, may prove useful:

"To win in disputes.

Then carry these staves on your left side and look at your adversary before he sees you, and say quietly: May my will grow and your victory go astray[60]."

Figure 66: Item 27, Lbs 764 8vo

As a final comment, anyone who genuinely wishes for a fair settlement rather than outright victory at all costs should consider making a prayer and an offering to Forseti, for, as it is written in the Gylfaginning section of the Prose Edda:

> "Forseti is the name of the son of Baldr and Nanna, Nep's daughter. He has a hall in heaven called Glitnir, and whoever comes to him with difficult legal disputes, they all leave with their differences settled. It is the best place of judgement among gods and men.[61]"

---

[60] The original words in Icelandic are more alliterative and rhyming: "Vaxi vilji minn en villist sigur þinn."
[61] Snorri Sturluson "Edda", translated by Anthony Faulkes, J.M. Dent & Sons Ltd, 1987

Brýnslustafir – keeping sharp is good

Who does not have at least a pocket knife close by them at all times? I know I do – a 'Swiss Army' one, with many different appliances, and very useful it is too. Some of my close friends, especially those who are interested in outdoor pursuits or historical re-enactment, are avid collectors of knives and swords. The evidence of the spell books shows that every Icelander would have his or her personal 'eating knife', which would probably be called upon for other minor tasks in addition to eating or carving magical staves. More important still was the use of scythes to cut hay quickly while the weather was good so that an adequate supply could be laid aside for the winter. The Icelandic summer is notoriously short and good weather is far from guaranteed, so the ability to use a scythe quickly and easily was extremely important. A tool made of good carbon steel will develop a very sharp edge, but it can also blunt quickly with use; hence it is essential to constantly hone it using a whetstone.

The whetstone is replete with mythical and magical significance. Whetstones feature in Odin's journey to retrieve the Holy Mead and Thor's battle with the giant Hrungnir. The folklorist Jacqueline Simpson has even drawn a connection with the Germanic sky-god Tiwaz. Ornate examples have been found among the grave goods of kings, and the very language associated with the tool – whet, hone, sharpen etc. – has been used metaphorically in a number of

Germanic languages to describe actions that positively influence states of mind and feeling[62].

A whetstone that had been magically 'charged' so that it would put a better and more lasting edge on a scythe would therefore have been extremely desirable. As only three such spells can be found in the six books of magic dealt with here, all three are given below.

From Lbs 2413 8vo:

> "If you want the edge of your scythe to stay sharp, carve these staves with your eating knife on your whetstone."

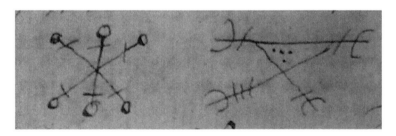

Figure 67: Item 137, Lbs 2413 8vo

From Lbs 764 8vo:

> "Whetstone magic. Carve these staves on the whetstone and sharpen three times, and read the following verse over [it] as you do so: Sator, Arepo, Tenet, Opera, Rotas."

---

[62] See Stephen A. Mitchell "The Whetstone as a Symbol of Authority in Old English and Old Norse" at www.academia.edu.

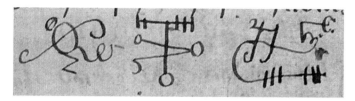

Figure 68: Item 17, Lbs 764 8vo

From ÍB 383 4to 'Huld':

"Carve the upper stave on top of your whetstone and the other below it. Lay some grass over it for a while. Then sharpen facing away from the sun and do not look at the edge."

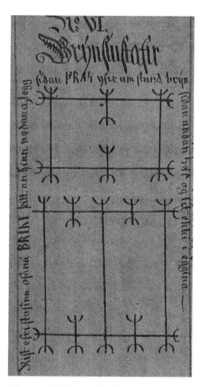

Figure 69: Item VI from Huld MS

The second and third spells incorporate some interesting peculiarities. The second one uses the words from the SATOR square, which was popular throughout Europe from the Middle Ages onward. In Iceland, it was used in a number of spells and credited with diverse powers such as curing headaches, easing childbirth, releasing snagged fishing tackle from the sea bed and averting evil, as well as enhancing the efficiency of a whetstone. The third spell is interesting because it treats the whetstone, after the staves have been carved on it, as a sentient wight in its own right: grass is laid over it for a while, as if to tell it what its ultimate purpose is (to aid in the mowing of hay), and it is to be used facing away from the sun, as if the bright sunlight might drive out or otherwise hamper the operation of the whetstone-spirit; furthermore, the person using it should not look at the edge of the scythe, but have faith in the stone to do its work.

So if these spells have *whetted* your appetite and you are *keen* to try them out, you might like to carve some staves on your favourite whetstone and find out whether they help to keep your edged tools sharp!

CHAPTER 10

THE ISSUE OF COMPLEXITY

Many examples of magical workings have been cited in the previous chapters, and the reader may well have already gained the impression that Icelandic magic was a very rough-and-ready affair that generally only called for the carving of one or more staves, perhaps combined with a short incantation. While it is certainly true that the majority of the operations listed in the grimoires give this impression, it is worth repeating that such books of magic are most likely personal aide-memoires that record only the salient points and omit details that the sorcerer may have deemed too obvious to write down. However, the spells were occasionally recorded with a fairly high degree of complexity. Some of them have already been referred to, so for the sake of brevity we will focus on two that have only been touched upon so far.

Firstly, the spell in 'Lækningakver' to magically charm a set of dice:

> "If you want to win at dice-playing, take your dice and bury them to the north of the churchyard for three nights, for three more nights to the south, and three to the east. Then place them on the altar under the cloth for three Masses. Then throw them up

185

with your hands with these words: 'I invoke you, Thor and Odin, by Christ the crucified, that you transfigure these dice'. And throw them up a second time and say: 'I invoke you by Enoch and Elijah'. And on the third time: 'I invoke you by Frigg and Freyja, by Thor and Odin, and by the holy virgin lady Saint Mary, that you, Fjolnir, let fall that which I can throw'."

One can see at a glance that there are numerous factors of time, location, direction, repetition and appeals to higher power involved in this working. Most of the action – if not all of it – takes place in and around the church: a sacred and powerful place. Some careful planning would have to go into this so as to avoid being discovered, and there would always be an element of risk. First the dice are buried to the north of the churchyard, the quarter associated with midnight and 'evil' in Christian belief, but with the Pole Star and the world-axis in Heathen belief; there they are to lie for 3 nights, presumably to gestate and absorb the powers of darkness. Then they are exhumed and re-buried to the south of the churchyard for another 3 nights, the quarter of the midday sun, presumably to absorb the powers of light and energy. Then they are taken again to the eastern side of the churchyard, the quarter of the rising sun (and, in Christian thought, of resurrection) for another 3 nights. Note that the west side, the quarter of the setting sun, is avoided; no element of decline is needed and the purpose of the working to load the dice, not balance them. The dice are then secreted under the altar cloth inside the church so that three masses will be unwittingly said over them by the priest, thereby 'consecrating' them. After all this has been done, they are retrieved and thrice cast into the air with evocations of higher powers, both Heathen and Christian, to 'activate' the dice.

The recurrence of the sacred and powerful number three can be clearly seen in the various stages and in the triangular journey made by the dice, terminating at the centre. Three is an 'odd' number and, unlike the square or the circle, the triangle represents dynamism and is not evenly balanced – exactly the kind of effect desired in the dice. The wording of the final phrase is telling: "...that you, Fjolnir, let fall that which I can throw" (*ath þu Fiolnir falla latir þat, er ec kasta kan*); the gambler does not ask that the dice consistently give a high score but rather what he needs. After all, some games require a certain number to result, not necessarily the highest possible. This is interesting for (apart from having the will to perform the working at all) it is only after all has been done that the sorcerer's own will comes into effect. Everything else is achieved by the mystical significance of geographical orientation, of number, and of the ritual performed by the Christian priest. Even when Thor and Odin are invoked, it is "by Christ the crucified"; in turn, Frigg and Freyja are invoked "by Thor and Odin, and by the holy virgin lady Saint Mary". It is as if, in this long and complex operation, the sorcerer has little confidence in his own power and ability, relying instead on tricking the parish priest into performing a major part of the ritual for him. This lack of confidence may possibly say a great deal about the mindset that needs such a complex procedure. Contrast, for example, the lengthy preparations and complicated procedures of magic in the Western (read 'Mediterranean') Tradition with the simpler spells in these grimoires or, indeed, with the magic of Egill Skallagrímsson. In the former, the magician essentially considers himself devoid of personal power, though not of knowledge; it is by his 'art' that he employs the various names of God and Christ to command angels and demons to do his bidding. In the latter, the magician appears to rely more on his own might and main, augmented and focused by the power of the runes or magical staves.

The second complex working that we shall consider here was recorded about a hundred years later in the Stockholm MS. It is a thief-finding spell but, unlike the general run of such workings, it does not rely on oneiromancy or scrying.

> "To find out a thief. If, with magical knowledge, you want to find out who is stealing from you, then take a little thorn bush and carry it on your person so that it may not be separated from you. Then take a little copper pin with a copper hammer. Make the following stave on the crossbeam of the house from which was stolen, then stick the pin into the right eye [of the figure], and while doing this say: 'In Buskan Lucanus'.

The stave: [See Figure 70 below]

Then say: Fortum atum est[63].

Write this stave on a crossbeam with chalk. The hammer is to be cast together with its shaft out of [metal] which has never been used before, out of unstamped copper and brass, when the sun is at its zenith."

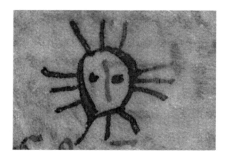

Figure 70: Stave from item 44 in Stockholm MS

This spell is fascinating for a multitude of reasons, not least because it was written in two separate hands: the portion of the text beginning "Write this stave on a crossbeam…" is a later addition by a successive owner of the same grimoire. This makes it clear that, in the seventeenth century at least, the magical knowledge was still being refined and added to. To consider this operation properly, we must first sort out the correct sequence of the procedures and the import of much of the wording. To begin with, something has been stolen and we do not know who the thief is. We could try to detect the thief's identity by

---

[63] As Flowers points out, probably a corruption of "Consummatum est" – "It is finished".

dreaming or scrying, as in so many other spells, but in this case a different course is taken. First, the victim takes a "little thorn bush" and carries it on his person in such a way that that it cannot come loose. The next thing is to draw the stave, with chalk, on the crossbeam of the house from which the goods were stolen. Note the wording here: not "your house" or "your barn" but "the house from which was stolen". This implies the possibility that the sorcerer may well be working on someone else's behalf, which is rife with social implications in the seventeenth century. This implication can only be confirmed by what follows. Having drawn the stave, which resembles a very simplistic human face with nine 'spokes' emanating from it, the sorcerer is to take a copper pin and drive it into the right eye of the figure using a hammer, a very special hammer made of copper (or brass) that has been cast from virgin metal (i.e. not scrap, never used before), saying "In Buskan Lucanus" as he does so, and ending with "Fortum atum est".

The first issue is the significance of the thorny bush, which must be carried. Why should this be done? It might be to harness the power of the thorn-rune and its power of retribution, gearing up the psyche of the sorcerer for the task ahead. On the other hand, thorn bushes, like mazes and lattices, are often considered potent traps for spirits, and it is possible that the sorcerer, wearing the said thorns and with his mind focused on retribution, hopes somehow to catch the soul of the miscreant in his daily doings and wanderings[64].

---

[64] I have heard that such methods are employed among the Zulu people of South Africa. If someone dies far from his native

Or it may be that something has been omitted here, and the intention is to trap local land-wights and compel them into cooperating with the working.

Next, let us consider the ownership of the tools. Iceland in the early modern period was destitute to a degree that we only associate with the very poorest countries of the 'third world' today[65]. People considered themselves fortunate to have ordinary, practical tools for the everyday purposes of mowing hay, cutting turf and slaughtering sheep, and I doubt very much that a copper foundry or raw copper were to be found anywhere on the island. A hammer made all of one piece "of unstamped copper and brass" when the sun was at her zenith would truly be a remarkable and expensive work of artifice. In fact, the making of such a tool could probably only be accomplished by travelling to another country such as England. Even copper pins would have been a rarity, having little practical use and being mainly used in decorative items. Furthermore, there is the matter of timing: the hammer must be made when the sun is at its zenith,

---

territory, in the mines of Johannesburg for example, a relative is sent with a sprig of buffalo-thorn to the place where the family member has died. The sprig is waved around, accompanied by certain ceremonies, to catch the spirit, and then conveyed back to the dead person's home ground. They will even pay for a place for the bush on one of the 'black taxis' (small buses) that are the commonest mode of transport for those that can afford them, and nobody among the other passengers will think anything unusual of this.

[65] For a good impression of life in 'old' Iceland, written in a very light-hearted but accurate way, read Alda Sigmundsdóttir "The Little Book of Icelanders in the Old Days", Enska textasmidjan 2014.

which implies that the magician himself has to make it or at least supervise the making. In short, this would have been a priceless tool that was passed down from generation to generation. It was certainly not something to be casually made in response to a recent case of theft. This, taken together with the aforementioned wording "…of the house from which was stolen", tends to imply that the services of professional or semi-professional sorcerers were in demand.

Finally, this working differs from most other thief-finding operations in its element of compulsion. Unlike the oneiromantic and scrying spells, it seeks to inflict pain on the thief, forcing him to reveal himself and perhaps return the stolen goods. This is confirmed by a separate but similar account in Jacqueline Simpson's book "Icelandic Folk Tales and Legends":

> "If a man owns a 'Thor's Hammer', he will know who it is who has robbed him if he loses anything. To make this hammer, one must have copper from a church bell, three times stolen. The hammer must be hardened in human blood on a Whitsunday, between the reading of the Epistle and the Gospel. A spike must also be forged out of the same material as the hammer, and this spike one must jab against the head of the hammer, saying: 'I drive this in the eye of the Father of War, I drive this in the eye of the Father of the Slain, I drive this in the eye of Thor of the Aesir.' The thief will then feel pain in his eyes; if he does not return the stolen goods, the procedure is repeated and then the thief will lose one eye; but should it prove necessary to repeat it a third time, he will lose the other eye too.

Another method is for a man to steal a copper bell from a church between the Epistle and the Gospel, and make a hammer from it. When he wants to know who the thief is, he must take a sheet of paper and draw a man's eyes on it, or, better still, a whole face with two eyes, using his own blood, and on the reverse of the sheet draw a suitable magic sign. Next, he must take a steel spike and set one end of it on the eye and strike the other end with the Thor's Hammer, saying 'I am giving eye-ache to the man who robbed me', or 'I am knocking out the eye of the man who robbed me'. Then the thief will lose one eye, or both, if he does not give himself up first.[66]"

The same eye-piercing motif can be seen in this 'Thor's Hammer' item from the Huld manuscript.

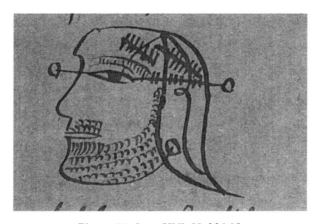

Figure 71: Item XVI, Huld MS

---

[66] Jacqueline Simpson "Icelandic Folktales and Legends", London 1972, pp. 181-182.

In conclusion, we have two very different magical operations that are both characterised by a degree of complexity. The first (the dice-loading spell) is performed by someone who is prepared to take a certain amount of risk but mainly trusts to other powers – the mystical significance of the compass quadrants, the sacred location, the power of the unwitting priest, and the invoked deities – to charm his dice so that they will fall as he wills. The second is most probably performed by a (semi-)professional sorcerer who owns specialised magical equipment and has the knowledge to use it. He would obviously have to be known among the local community to be called in for the resolution of the theft problem, and would no doubt also be called upon to perform other services or give advice of a magical nature. While magical praxis in Iceland may mainly have been characterised by its ad hoc nature, it could nevertheless involve a great deal of planning, preparation and meticulous timing on occasions.

CHAPTER 11

CONCLUSIONS

In the preceding chapters, we have examined many of the elements that characterise magic as it was practised in Iceland in the early modern period; even so, this really constitutes no more than a lightning tour based on only six extant manuscripts. There are still many other manuscripts to be researched and many other factors to be considered. These, however, will have to be the subject of subsequent papers and publications. Now it is time to bring together all that has been learned so far, to summarise the aims and techniques, and to attempt to answer the question raised in the introduction: what defines Icelandic magic and sets it apart from other traditions?

Who practised magic, and with what intentions?

Although the Icelandic folk tales and legends tend to emphasise the activities of certain ordained clerics and their attendance at a certain 'Black School' in Paris, the magic of the grimoires is mainly of a very 'folksy' nature which, it seems, could be practised by just about anyone – at least as regards the simpler workings. There is no mention in the grimoires of a requirement for intensive training beforehand, although this cannot be ruled out simply because it is not mentioned. As stated in chapter 1, Iceland has long enjoyed widespread vernacular literacy and it is the only country where the possession of books of magic features significantly in the records of witchcraft trials. This implies that access to magical knowledge in written form was not the sole preserve of an educated aristocracy or priestly class. Indeed, the tenor and purposes of many of the spells seem designed to appeal mainly to people of the less privileged classes.

The wording and preoccupations of the grimoires, together with the trial records, indicate that sorcery was mainly a male occupation, which runs counter to the perception of the folk magician in other countries, where 95% of those convicted of 'witchcraft' were women. Today we can only speculate as to why this was so; it may have been because of the male-dominated nature of Icelandic society, in which sexual discrimination was rife. As in many other societies, even much later in history, it may have been that literacy was viewed as less necessary for women than for men.

While many of the spells of which we have details could be performed by anyone, a careful reading of the sub-text shows that very specialised equipment might be required on occasions. Such is the nature of this that we can only conclude that there must have been some people who devoted a great deal of time and expense to the magical arts, and may have been virtually full-time sorcerers with dedicated magical toolkits. This being so, it is unlikely that they needed these things purely to ensure that their own lives proceeded according to plan, nor could they have maintained such a lifestyle without the benefit of surplus time, which can only mean that they sold their services to others in return for food and other necessities.

The aims of the workings in the grimoires are overwhelmingly prosaic, dealing mainly with mundane concerns of day-to-day survival and prosperity. There are spells for healing humans and livestock, for exposing thieves, for love and seduction, for getting a good harvest of hay or a good catch of fish, for luck and popularity; in short, the eternal and ubiquitous preoccupations of thaumaturgy. Even the spells intended to harm by magic or to protect against such harm can be counted as 'mundane' in a world where no clear distinction was drawn between the 'natural' and the 'supernatural'. The element that is clearly lacking in the grimoires is that of personal, transformational development in the alchemical tradition. Unlike the Renaissance magicians of mainland Europe, Icelandic magicians seem to have evinced no curiosity regarding the hidden workings of the universe, let alone used their arts to reveal such 'mysteries'. There is perhaps one single exception to this in all of these six grimoires, a spell contained in Lbs 2413 8vo:

> "If you want to know what is hidden from the common man. Carve these staves on brass with steel and lay by your ear, and fall asleep, and you will experience."

Figure 72: Item 100, Lbs 2413 8vo

(Note that the word used for 'experience' is *reyna*, the same verb used in the Rune Gild's motto *Reyn til Runa*.)

Of course, it is possible that the magicians of Iceland had managed, throughout a shorter period of Christianity than experienced by their continental brethren, to maintain an indigenous transcendental view of the universe and hence had no need of theurgy. However, given the pervasive influence of Christian teachings that can be seen even in the grimoires, this seems unlikely.

Techniques and tools – summary

As we have seen in chapter 4, Icelandic magic in this period employed three main techniques:

a) The carving of a stave, or staves (sometimes with the addition of blood or spittle);

b) Incantation;

c) Appeals to a supernatural power.

In this respect, it differed little from some of the magical operations described in the saga literature and indicated by archaeological finds. Indeed, it is entirely possible that the 'runes' referred to in the saga literature were more like the *galdrastafir* shown in the preceding chapters than the Futhark runes, though the archaeological evidence tends to militate against this theory. Quite often, these three techniques were used in combination, but they might also be used singly or in pairs. Rarely, however, does one encounter an appeal to supernatural powers on its own; even those workings in the grimoires that are denoted as 'prayers' have an element of incantation about them. What is absolutely clear is the primacy of image-magic: the vast majority of the spells include a magical stave, an image or some form of runes as an integral part of the working.

The preferred methods of delivering the intention were by contact or proximity, although some spells appear to have worked at a distance from their target. The tools that were used varied from extremely simple, such as a finger wetted with spittle or one's personal knife, to rare and costly items that had to be specially made, or which might only be occasionally chanced upon. One can well imagine the devoted sorcerer amassing a treasured tool-kit and supplementing it as necessary: a copper Thor's Hammer that has been passed down from generation to generation; likewise, a copper knife, an awl of lead and another of silver; scraps of lead, copper and brass; pieces of baleen and the hide from a heifer's first calf; feathers and skin from specific birds; and last, but not least, a human skull and other bones exhumed from a burial place.

On occasion, and perhaps more often than immediately implied in the instructions of the grimoires, the Icelandic magician would try to align the timing of his operations with the motions of the sun, the moon and the tides, with certain days of the week and with certain feast-days. We have only a few examples in the manuscripts reviewed in the present work, but it is entirely possible that the knowledge presented by these may be expanded with examination of other material and with a thorough examination of the folklore. The same applies to mentions of geographical alignment, location and direction of movement. Though the data is fragmented and hard to come by, it indicates that time, space and direction were sometimes important in aligning the intention with the broader motions of the cosmos.

It is now time to respond to the big, difficult question lurking behind these details: what view of *magical causality* did the Icelandic sorcerers have as they plied their magic? In other words, how did they think their magic worked, if indeed they thought about it at all? In truth, they probably did not trouble themselves very much about such issues. If the magic worked, that was all there was to it, and magicians of all ages have relied greatly on the antiquity of spells as evidence of their efficacy. However, it is a question which modern practitioners of magic, steeped in the spirit of post-Enlightenment scientific enquiry must ask, even as we rebel against bland, scientific rationalism.

Reading between the lines of the spells, it would appear that the first component of the magic is the magician's own will, intent and emotion; this is the bedrock on which the entire procedure is founded. Some instructions are quite specific concerning the state of mind to be adopted: "Have strong faith"; "Keep a strong faith"; "Say what you desire with anger", and "Think well on that which was stolen before you sleep". Other instructions seem designed to sharpen the mind of the magician and keep him focused on the operation; for example, "Do not say your prayers". This would deny the magician a routine ritual to bring the day to a comfortable close, ensuring that his sleep would be disturbed by the divinatory dreams that he desired. The same applies to injunctions to perform magical workings while fasting, as hunger would focus the mind and introduce an element of self-sacrifice.

The second component is the stave-form (or forms in the case of multiple staves). It is clear that a high degree of confidence is invested in the power of the staves to convert the subjective will of the magician into objective reality. The belief appears to have been that the staves embody and channel extra-personal forces in their own right, forces that exist somewhere beyond the normal continuum of space and time. When the will of the magician is directed and invested in these staves through carving (or even by visualisation in the case of some helm-of-awe) workings), they become activated and function both as accumulators and transmitters of power. The preference for transmission of the magical intent by contact or close proximity demonstrates a perception that the charged staves generally radiate their power, and the intent invested in them, over a finite physical distance on the earthly plane rather like radio beacons. However, they do not radiate this power simply to anyone who happens to be around them, but only to the designated receptor. In addition, the power of the stave can be enhanced by the application of body fluids, usually the magician's own blood or saliva but sometimes that of an animal[67]. The possible rationale for this is two-fold: firstly, blood is symbolic of the life-force and its application therefore brings the stave to life on the physical plane; secondly, the magician's own blood or saliva are infused with his will and are used as a vehicle to transfer that will and combine it the power of the stave.

The third component is incantation, *galdur* in the original meaning of the word. Belief in the power of the spoken word to change objective reality is a very ancient one, common to many different traditions. In Nordic magic, from the earliest records onwards, the power of the word is enhanced and refined by forming words into rhyming and alliterative chants, and this tradition persisted in the early modern period.

The final component is an appeal to a supernatural power – God, Christ, the Devil, the old Nordic deities etc. – for assistance, but this appears to be regarded as largely dispensable in comparison with the pre-eminence of the magical stave. Only in 50 cases out of a total of 360 is there an appeal to a supernatural power without the use of a magical sign or image, compared with 224 cases in which a magical sign or image is used without any appeal to a supernatural power.

---

[67] According to records of the witchcraft trials, semen was also used, but no mention of it is made in any of these six grimoires.

To sum up, it would appear that the magicians of Iceland believed in their power to change objective reality by will. The will was heightened and focused by maintaining a certain emotional state and by physical practices such as fasting, then transferred to a magical symbol that served to accumulate, augment and transmit the intention, often by contact with the recipient but also over a certain physical radius. The willed intention was then defined and empowered once again by the utterance or singing of certain words, often in poetic form, at some point in the procedure but usually just after the carving of the stave. The fact that certain instruments are prescribed for carving, and certain materials for carving on, indicates a belief that these materials are somehow more receptive to certain intentions than to others. Unfortunately, however, it has not been possible to draw up any consistent 'table of correspondences' when working with this small data base.

The construction of the staves – can any sense be made of this?

Another issue that fascinates and tantalises present-day magicians is the construction of these intriguing magical staves. What do they symbolise? By what processes are they assembled? Are they derived from the Futhark runes? And is it possible to analyse them and extract rules by which new staves for different purposes may be invented? This is a question that I am working on together with an Australian researcher, Justin Foster. Some writers have already attempted this task. Working from the a priori assumption that the Icelandic magical staves must be complex binds, derived from the Futhark runes and built up in a process similar to the 'sigilization' developed by modern Chaos magicians, they then twist and bend the facts to suit the theory. The results, predictably, are unconvincing. Even a brief scan of the most extensive grimoire that is available as a translated and published work, Lbs 2413 8vo, shows that there is too much variation for this to be the case. Often, very different staves are prescribed in separate spells for exactly the same purpose. Sometimes, identical staves are used for very different purposes. In short, there is no consistency of the kind one would expect to emerge if an underlying system based on the Futhark runes existed. Furthermore, similar forms have emerged in other cultures through the ages; cultures with no established connection with the Futhark. For instance, tablets containing symbols very similar to the *ægishjálmur* have been found on the Persian Gulf island of Failaka, and similar motifs are a recurring feature in traditional Croatian tattoos.

This is not to say that we should give up trying to interpret the staves and to discern some underlying pattern in them, only that we will probably have to cast our net much wider than the Futhark runes when seeking the conceptual symbolism that determines their structure. Of course, this is very visual exercise. I have made a small start by pasting the stave images onto small, blank cards, together with their provenance and a few words describing their purpose, to facilitate comparison of the images from different grimoires (and on different pages of the same grimoire). However, this is a long and laborious task when hundreds of images are involved, and we may have to look to computer software designed for image recognition and comparison to speed up the process.

Final conclusion: how are we to typify Icelandic magic?

In order to define Icelandic magic, to mark out the factors that make it special, we must first define what it is not. Firstly there is no indication of diabolism whatsoever in the records of the witchcraft trials or in the evidence of the grimoires, except where – occasionally – the Devil, Satan or Beelzebub are called upon. Even when these Christian demonic entities are evoked, it is usually in the company of God, Christ, the Holy Trinity or of pre-Christian, Heathen gods. There are no accounts of nocturnal flights (mainly by women) to mountain locations for the purpose of holding demonic Sabbaths, no pacts with the Judeo-Christian 'Devil'. In short, none of the usual deeds and rituals so typical of what was considered 'witchcraft' in mainland Europe during the sixteenth and seventeenth centuries. Furthermore, there is in Icelandic magic very little of the sympathetic magic, involving the use of poppets, hair, nail clippings etc. that one encounters in tales of European witchcraft. At the other end of the spectrum, we do not see the kind of 'Christian Cabbalism' that characterised the searching of the educated (and hence very often ordained) élite in the same period. There seems to be a profound difference in philosophy and concept of personal power at play here. The European Renaissance magician, by comparison with the Icelandic magician, seems to have perceived himself as relatively powerless in his own right, entirely dependent on his knowledge or 'arts' to command other entities to do his bidding from the safe confines of a protective circle.

By contrast, Icelandic magic appears to have been very much the preserve of males, in particular (judging from the wording of many spells) males of the underclass, of poor crofters, servants and field-hands. It would seem that, in many instances, the spells could be used by any who had access to them. On the other hand, the sophistication of the equipment indicates that there may have been a class of hereditary sorcerers whose services were called upon by others in the community in time of need. In keeping with the strong tradition of vernacular literacy and the reverence for books in general, the ownership of a personal grimoire was something to be prized, even if it did bring certain risks in the face of persecution by the Crown authorities. There was, with some few exceptions, no evocation of demons or even of angels to carry out the errand of the magician. Nor was there any need to cast a protective circle, for the magician does not appear to have felt threatened by the forces that he evoked. What really counted in magic was his own will, on occasions brought into alignment with the forces of the cosmos by virtue of timing, location and direction of movement, but mainly augmented and transmitted by combination with a magical stave and a well-crafted piece of incantation. In this respect, one can discern a direct line of continuity with the magic of the saga accounts and a tradition that is very different from anything to be found in mainland Europe.

I do hope that you, the reader, have enjoyed reading this work. Please feel free to contact me via the publisher with regard to any errors, omissions or helpful suggestions.

WORKS CITED

Primary sources

AM 434 a 12mo 'Lækningakver', Arnamagnæan Institute, Copenhagen

ATA, Amb 2, F 16:26 'Galdrabók' (referred to throughout as the 'Stockholm MS'), Antiquarian Topographical Archive, Stockholm

Lbs 143 8vo 'Galdrakver', Icelandic National and University Library

Lbs 2413 8vo, Icelandic National and University Library

Lbs 764 8vo, Icelandic National and University Library

ÍB 383 4to 'Huld', Icelandic National and University Library

Secondary sources

"Three Icelandic Outlaw Sagas", Viking Society for Northern Research 2004

Alda Sigmundsdóttir "The Little Book of Icelanders in the Old Days", Enska textasmidjan 2014

Ben Waggoner "Norse Magical and Herbal Healing", The Troth, New Haven (Connecticut) 2011

Christopher A. Smith "The Icelandic Tradition of Magic: Analysis of a Late Eighteenth-Century Icelandic Galdrabók", published in "Occult Traditions", Numen Books 2011

Francois-Xavier Dillmann, "Les Magiciens dans l'Islande Ancienne", Uppsala 2006

Gisli Sigurðsson, "Oral sagas, poems and lore" in "The Manuscripts of Iceland", Reykjavík 2004

Jacqueline Simpson "Icelandic Folktales and Legends", London 1972

Jochum Magnús Eggertsson ('Skuggi') "Galdraskræða", Lesstofan, Reykjavík 2013

Jón R. Hjálmarsson, "History of Iceland from the Settlement to the Present Day", 3rd edition, Reykjavík 2007

Justin Foster, "The Huld Manuscript - ÍB 383 4to: A modern transcription, decryption and translation", www.academia.edu, June 2015

Magnús Rafnsson, "Angurgapi. The Witch-hunts in Iceland", Strandagaldur, Hólmavík 2003

Magnús Rafnsson, "Tvær Galdraskræður. Two Icelandic Books of Magic", Strandagaldur, Hólmavík 2008

Owen Davies "Grimoires. A History of Magic Books", OUP, Oxford 2009

Richard Kieckhefer, "Magic in the Middle Ages", Canto Edition, Cambridge University Press, Cambridge 2000

Snorri Sturluson "Edda", translated by Anthony Faulkes, J.M. Dent & Sons Ltd, 1987

Soffía Guðný Guðmundsdóttir and Laufey Guðnadóttir, "Book production in the Middle Ages" in "The Manuscripts of Iceland", Reykjavík 2004

Stephen A. Mitchell, "Leechbooks, Manuals, and Grimoires. On the early History of Magical Texts in Scandinavia" available at www.academia.edu

Stephen A. Mitchell, "Witchcraft and Magic in the Nordic Middle Ages", University of Pennsylvania Press, Philadelphia 2011

Stephen E. Flowers, Ph.D., "The Galdrabók", 2nd revised edition, Runa-Raven Press, Smithville (TX) 2005

The Poetic Edda, translation by Lee M. Hollander, University of Texas Press 1962

Thröstur Eysteinsson "Forestry in a treeless land", Icelandic Forest Service, Egillsstaðir, 2009

SUGGESTIONS
FOR FURTHER READING

- "Icelandic Magic Symbols (galdrastafir) and Spell Books (galdrabækur) - An Annotated English Translation" by Justin Foster. www.academia.edu , 2015.

- "Icelandic Magic: The Mystery and Power of the Galdrabok Grimoire" by Stephen E. Flowers (projected publication date 22/01/2016)

- "Trolldom: spells and methods of the Norse folk magic tradition" by Johannes Gardback, 2015.

- "Sorcerer's Screed" (an English translation of Skuggi's 'Galdraskræða'), Lesstofan, 2015.

INDEX

PUBLISHED BY AVALONIA

www.avaloniabooks.co.uk

Lightning Source UK Ltd.
Milton Keynes UK
UKOW02f1121291015

261650UK00003B/328/P

9 781905 297931